ENTERING
the
WILD

ENTERING
the
WILD

Essays on Faith and Writing

a memoir by
JEAN JANZEN

Good Books

Intercourse, PA 17534
800/762-7171
www.GoodBooks.com

Acknowledgments

My thanks to the editors of the following journals in which some of these essays appeared: *Conrad Grebel Review, Cross Currents, Mennonite Life, Pacific Journal,* and *Rhubarb.*

Special thanks to Meredith Kunsa who read and gave suggestions for most of the essays, and to Jeff Gundy and Julia Kasdorf for their help and encouragement along the way.

Design by Cliff Snyder

ENTERING THE WILD

Copyright © 2012 by Good Books, Intercourse, PA 17534
International Standard Book Number: 978-1-56148-757-8
Library of Congress Control Number: 2012940821

Publisher's Cataloging-in-Publication Data

Janzen, Jean.
Entering the wild : essays on faith and writing / a memoir by Jean Janzen.
p. cm.
ISBN 978-1-56148-757-8 (pbk.)

1. Janzen, Jean. 2. Mennonite women --Biography.
3. Mennonite authors --Biography. I. Title.

BX8141 .J36 2012
289.7/092/2 --dc23   2012940821

Contents

1

Roar and Stillness:

California as Home

1957 to the Present

IT IS THE MIDDLE OF THE NIGHT, THIS NO-TIME when I awaken unsure of where I am for a moment. Then the senses retrace it all once again. It is June into summer mode. Jasmine's last blossoms, no breeze, the air of desert valley, dry with its sharp drop into night chill. Stillness with a small roar of creek water over a weir two houses away. Now a rustle of palm leaves, a screech owl calling. The smell of dust. It's home.

How did I get here, and how have I managed to stay in one house for more than forty years, the child of immigrants who moved me from Canada to the Midwestern United States, who lived in fifteen different houses in the first thirty years of my life? Still married to the same man. Four children, seven grandchildren. Writing poetry in this roar and silence. I take a breath and retrace some more.

Back to Saskatchewan, where in my first months I am sheltered from the blizzards by six siblings in a teacherage. Back to the Ukraine, where my father lies on a dirt floor and listens to his father play the violin he made. Back to my mother's Minnesota home, where her brothers discuss theology and plow black soil. They hold me holding these places, and when I leave, I carry them with me.

And when I marry and enter California, I spend my first night in the roar of Yosemite Falls. We arrive after nightfall, find a tent cabin, and gratefully lie down on cots, letting the sound of the June snowmelt cascade over us. It is an initiation of reverberation as the double falls crash into giant boulders and then churn their force into the valley's river, the steep granite walls echoing. To sleep in such tremendous noise is to give up to something new and powerful. Eight months pregnant with our first child, the mild cramping I feel is more than a warning. My life is about to change.

Not that it is my first roar, but this is new. It's not the thunder and tornado of the Midwest. Or World War II, or the revivalist preachers. This is the sound of an abundance that asks for awe. I have met the majesty of the mountains. I am about to live in a place where wilderness overpowers agriculture. Instead of me owning the land, marking it off neatly and cultivating it, the land seems to own me.

We spend three years in the Los Angeles basin while my husband does his medical training and two of our children are born. From there we move to this Great Central Valley, with its mountain ranges on either side, and beyond, in the west, the mysterious ocean. We have come to this state to try it for a year or two, and, like others, we stay. We find work, a children's hospital for my pediatrician husband, a Mennonite community, some relatives, and the grand scenery.

The transition is challenging. The wilderness encroaches and threatens with wildlife, with its dangerous river rapids and the possibility of becoming lost. I could lose the children. The culture is a roar with its boomtown mentality, flabby buildings, loose dust, its history and lack of it. The experimentation is exaggerated in the 1960s when the children are small. As they grow they are a part of it, loosening themselves in the rivers, yet seeking bedrock.

The roar is fearful and fertile. The falls pour through canals into our subtropical desert valley and allow cotton and grapes to thrive. The roar is in the peaches and plums. We eat it with juice running down our chins. It is in the aching back of migrant workers. It is in the poems I try to write. How shall we live in this place?

Stillness is a particular gift in this valley; the mountain ranges bordering it allow a high pressure buildup, subduing the winds and resulting in many days of calm. Summer clouds are mostly held away, and we are given a blue enameled sky day after day from May to November. These are the months of a hush that turns into deep velvet evenings and a cathedral for morning birdsong. This stalled air allows the sun to slam down with temperatures in the 90s and 100s, undisturbed. In the winter the fog nestles and stays for days.

Perhaps it is the combination of hush and grandeur that helps to translate fear into awe. The mountain offers its silence and its constancy, even as it breaks down for us, its granite and vegetation, and its snow-fields washing down into fertility. And so it offers me itself in the swelling grape and the fragility of the iris petal with its translucent purples and whites. It says, somehow, that holiness desires me.

California as place is a home of demand. Living in the presence of the mountains and a few hours away from the ocean's tireless tug on our coast is to become more than you are. Stand beside the giant sequoia red-wood trees, and you are convinced that you must live large. The way may be narrow, but the goal is wide. It is nothing less than God.

The Midwestern sky with its gifts and threats was an emblem of God in grace and judgment. That sky came with me to this place. But over there God could be controlled part of the time—by my good behavior, even by my belief. This California God continually asks for relinquishment; I am helpless.

So when I awaken in a June night by moth wing or my aging body, I am empty but not alone. My arms spread out in wonder that I am here. It is the posture I want to hold with my family, my church community, and my Fresno community. It is the way I must sit before the empty page to begin a poem. The night presses its immensity and mystery against me and knows me. It calls me by my name.

2

My Father's Joy:

How My Father's Search Shaped My Life

1939 to 1970

THE DAY OUR FAMILY ENTERED THE UNITED STATES from Canada, all the flags were out. It was June 14, 1939, my sister's fourteenth birthday, and my father teased her that the stars and stripes were in honor of her special day. We were traveling in two cars with drivers from the church in Mountain Lake, Minnesota, which had hired my father to be the new pastor. Nine of us in a heavy rainstorm that turned the gravel roads into mud, brown water splashing against the car windows, as though nature was testing our decision to immigrate.

At the age of forty-five, my father was switching vocations from country schoolteacher to become pastor of a Mennonite church. His joy in teaching the Bible as lay leader in the Saskatchewan church led to his decision; he also was weary of teaching eight grades in one room for more than twenty years. In addition, he and my mother were seeking, for their three oldest children, a high school education closer to home, which was not as available in the Dalmeny area of Saskatchewan, where we lived in the teacherage on the schoolyard out in the country.

Now we were becoming small-town dwellers in this undulating, green landscape, the streets shaded by maples, a park with a bandstand at the center surrounded by neatly kept stores. We claimed Mountain Lake without reservation. My oldest brother found a country school teaching position, and the fifty dollars a month salary from the church was padded with gifts of a cow, chickens, a smoked ham, and seeds for the garden. Three brothers and my oldest sister entered a flourishing public high school, complete with excellent choirs and a band, and my younger sister and I were students in Bible school, which once was called German school for its effort to preserve the mother tongue. In the church we were surrounded with kindness, new friendships, and familiar Mennonite ways of singing and learning.

I began kindergarten in the parochial school. It was a year filled with sensory images — much singing, an indoor sandbox, and the noise and enthusiasm of post-high school Bible students playing Ping-Pong in that same basement space. Outside we played fox and geese in the snow and pumped our legs on the swings until

we almost reached heaven. We heard Bible stories
illustrated on blackboards with colored chalk. Here
I learned both the English and German alphabets. I
wrote my first poems in grade four, encouraged by Miss
Rieger, then bound the five little poems with yarn from
my mother's knitting basket. We presented our voices
in memorized pieces and songs in elaborate programs.
In one of the Christmas programs little Samuel began
reciting the poem *"Ich bin so froh,"* (I am so joyful)
with quavering voice, then broke into sobs. The loving Miss Rieger carried his trembling body off-stage
as we all began to sing "Joy to the World." This event
became a source of laughter at our family supper table,
but I sensed its true meaning only later in life.

Our family move became more dramatic when our
newly adopted country entered the war. After months
of anxiety, my three older brothers, being draft age,
received deferments because they were ministerial
students. Blackouts, rationing, and battle reports from
the radio clouded our household. The revivalists who
came to our city to call sinners forward in this time
of danger added terror to my life. While my father
distrusted some of the ways of these evangelists, most
of the town seemed to be mesmerized by the drama
and skill of these preachers, whose music staff would
introduce such songs as "Blackout for Jesus" while the
local Buller twins hammered away at the marimba.

Soon after he began pastoring, my father became
aware that he needed more training, and so he began a
weekly commute to Minneapolis for Bible courses. He

would take the bus on Monday and return on Thursday full of enthusiasm for his professors and studies. After his arrival from the bus depot, too late for our family supper, mother fried eggs and potatoes for him, and I would stand beside him as he ate, listening to his summaries and his joy, smelling the romance of cigarette smoke on his clothes and hair. Somehow the worldliness and sacred writings combined into something adventurous and wonderful, even as it was a confusion of what was forbidden and what was holy.

My father's passion for learning moved us in 1945 to Kansas, where he joined two of his children at Tabor College to gain his own bachelor's degree. This displacement just before sixth grade was jarring—a new public school, new friends, and a house full of college men where my parents were in charge. Twelve, going on thirteen, I was thrust into a "family" of college men who pounded up and down the stairs and had late-night escapades unheard of in our household. On this college campus I was exposed to the beauty of choral singing in the stained glass chapel, a taste of faith and the arts coming together, and witnessed the apparent joy of intellectual discussion as my father shared ideas and concerns with my siblings and fellow students.

Sometimes at supper, overwhelmed by his required courses, he would sigh and confess that he might not pass his class in genetics. I worried with him and for my sister struggling with new friends and geometry, and my little brother needing home-schooling after breaking a leg on the school playground. In this town I wrestled with the invitation to sing the lead role in "Hansel and Gretel." My parents allowed me, now a sixth-grader, to decide, and my piety won out. This was too much like the forbidden theater; I would be a brave soldier for Jesus and give it up. Even now I ache a little when I hear Humperdinck's heavenly duet, "When at night I go to sleep, fourteen angels watch do keep," either for the beauty of it, or, who knows, the lost chance of a stage career.

On weekends my parents took us three younger ones with them to a house church in a town about twenty miles away where ten or fifteen people gathered to be taught the "true" Mennonite faith. Here I took catechism from my father. With his gentle teaching, I assented to the gospel without reservation, willing to "accept Jesus as my personal savior and to follow him," yet I was terrified that I might be killed in a car crash on the narrow country roads on our way home at night. My baptism was arranged in special circumstances—we were moving back to Minnesota, where our church performed the ritual by pouring water over the head. The Mennonite Brethren (M.B.) required total immersion, and chances were that at Tabor College one day I might meet an M. B. to marry. Therefore, my father arranged for my minister-brother to immerse me in very cold water in front of several witnesses. Sometimes I still gasp in the memory of that "political" decision.

Properly drenched, I entered eighth grade back among my Minnesota friends. The experiment with school administration was not satisfying to my father. After three years he returned to pastoring, moving us yet again from the Minnesota home, this time to western Kansas, where I completed my high school education. In the academy he became my Bible teacher, the role in which, in retrospect, he seemed most at ease. In this flat countryside I was also educated by dust, wind, and gorgeous sunsets, and by my father's shining face as he came out of his study to tell my mother about a new discovery.

Did my father's love of learning influence my own movement into poetry? Surely the songs, hymns, and poems of childhood, and the memorizing of passages in the King James Bible, were leaning me toward love of language. When I brought home report cards with straight A's, he would chuckle and stutter out the A-A-A's. What I wanted was his praise. When I won awards in school, my mother, instead of expressing her pleasure, would warn me "not to get proud." Yearning for approval, was I learning lessons for the long journey of life and writing, that joy waited in the process itself, that praise and knowledge are not bliss?

And what is joy? In his essay "A Manna for All Seasons," Anthony Esolen defines it as the Sabbath being present in the midst of labor. He describes a visit with his cousins in Italy who take the day off work to tramp through the woods with him to gather mushrooms for dinner. Like the gathering of manna, he writes. "We might say of joy itself, 'What is this thing?' because if we can work for it, it isn't."

Surely for me the "stabs of joy" have been granted in my marriage, in such events and gifts as the birth of our children, the restoration of friendship, and the assurance of being loved in a myriad of ways. Making an unexpected discovery in the process of writing has been a source of joy. Yet it is a state that cannot be sustained, so well stated by William Blake: "He who binds to himself a joy/ Does the winged life destroy/ But he who kisses the joy as if flies/ Lives in eternity's sunrise."

At our wedding (I did marry an M. B.) the pianist played "Jesu, Joy of Man's Desiring," Bach's wonderful setting of the text by Johann Schor, the confession that not even our marriage partner can offer ultimate bliss. We didn't know at the time that the sense of the original text had been lost in translation into English, lifting Jesus into a lofty abstract being. The original in German carries an intimacy and a kind of vow: "Jesus shall remain my joy, my heart's comfort, carrying all sorrow. He is my eyes' delight and sun, my soul's darling."

My father's devotion to my mother, and hers to him, was exemplary. He openly showed affection for her in our home, holding her on his lap and caressing her in our presence, something I rarely witnessed in the homes of others. They sustained each other in his quest for learning and vocation, and they accompanied major decisions with the words, "We have found the joy to do this."

Being the child of a pastor, however, was an education like no other. If I had left the church, it would have been over the poor treatment he at times received from his parishioners. The lack of skill and grace in lay leadership is a painful memory. He agonized mostly silently, or with my mother, who was his solace, although he honored me during my late high school and college years with some confidential complaints. But he also expressed gratitude when his parishioners showed evidence of growth and learning.

In his last days, my father was torn between wanting to go home to God, or home to his Anna. I arrived in his last hours when he was in a coma and restless, almost as if he had some learning left to do. I caressed him to soothe him, reciting the Twenty-Third Psalm. I wanted him to recognize and acknowledge me, but this was a journey he would take without me or my mother.

His peaceful, final breaths were holy, and at his funeral service we sang joyful hymns of gratitude through our tears.

3

Sleeping in the Cellar:

A Reclamation of Birthplace

1933 to 1982

I AM INSIDE MOTHER EARTH IN THIS NORTHERN midsummer, shivering under wool blankets, wearing two sweaters over my pajamas. This is Saskatchewan in July. I'm almost fifty and have returned after forty years to the place of my birth. Cousin Susie has offered me a guest bed in the basement of her house.

My mother will sleep upstairs where she and Susie are sharing memories of playing with cousins on summer evenings—homemade ice cream, the chunks of ice stored in a dry well on Uncle John's farm. The light still lingers in late evening. Cream fresh from the cows, my six brothers and sisters take turns churning the

ice-cream maker. This fertile farmland to which my
Grandfather Schultz brought his entire family—seven
sons and three daughters—in 1902 is the place of our
family reunion. Some of my ancestors are buried on
this land. Do their bodies ever thaw after the long win-
ters? I wonder.

My earliest memory is about warmth. I am sitting
in my older sister's lap, and we are rocking close to the
wood cookstove. My mother is frying potatoes. Nine of
us in a small teacherage that we later find preserved
and moved from the country to the little town of
Langham. But it is the cold that dominates—the tubs
of piled-high snow dumped into a black hole under
the porch floor for household water. The window my
mother melts out of ice with a flat iron so that I can
watch the school kids circle on the skating rink, my
father joining them. My baby brother's small coffin,
which my older brothers carry over the late April
snows. The covered sled rides with the neighbors,
horses pulling us to church over drifts, a small stove
jiggling, heavy wool blankets to our chins.

Here I am, underground, remembering. Or am I
rehearsing for burial under this ceiling, floorboards
creaking above me as the two older women reminisce
and walk about? Tree roots drink around me, aspen,
willows, the tunnels of moles. I could stay awhile,
open a jar of applesauce or beans, and be nourished by
Susie's canning labors stored in the next room. Potatoes
from last September's dig. Enough blankets to see me

through another winter. Insulated from my duties of wife, mother, volunteer, I could hibernate in the dark.

What lies buried here, however, wants to rise, to live. Fertility of the subconscious waits. Teilhard de Chardin writes that the whole earth is lit from within. I am, after all, sleeping closer to the original fire of this planet, the magma below, here where no volcanoes have erupted in recent millennia. Here where language waits, even first memories of arms, rocking chair, stove moving the imagination toward meaning, toward trust. Someone hearing me when I cry out to be held.

My baby brother Stanley, who lived only twelve days, lies nearby in the local cemetery, his grave unmarked. I want to buy a marker for him, for his name, the same cemetery where Great-Grandfather Klassen lies, the one who buried his sister en route from Prussia to Ukraine almost two hundred years ago. His daughter, Anna, my grandmother, lies nearby beside her husband Peter Schultz. Grandfather Peter, farmer/pastor whose pulpit I stood behind for a photo, his Bible in my hands, the one he took with him on his visitation rounds. He would interrupt the farmer's plowing, suggest that they let the horses rest as they sat down together to read the ancient poems: "The heavens declare the glory of God, and the earth proclaims his handiwork," lifting their weariness into the lightness of immensity.

Handiwork around me now, intricacies of roots and animals in a rich embroidery. Will I awaken in time to see the aurora borealis? Not until harvest, Susie says. But she is wrong this time. I sleep through a fine display, stay grounded in earthly dreams in language that seeks the rhythm of seasons and fertility. Here my father stepped off the train from Quebec, a fifteen-year-old orphan, and walked across a field to his older brother. His passport is in Russian, his spoken language a Dutch dialect. He will labor on the Buhler family farm near here to pay back his ship fare. He will study Chaucer, become a teacher. He will marry the darling of the village. After six children, my mother asks the doctor for birth-control advice, and he answers that he cannot give it; he is Catholic.

I, the seventh child, will visit Rome. I will see where the martyr, St. Peter, is buried and hear the stories of Christians hiding in cellars and caves. I will see the words on the walls, symbols becoming words, becoming life. My name is Jean, feminine for John, meaning grace of God. I am walking upstairs. I embrace my mother.

4

After the Wedding:

How Dramatic Beginnings Molded Our Marriage

1954 to the Present

> Our marriage
> light as a page
>
> a script of skin
> reading skin
>
> chapters glued
> together

> the book thickens
> as it lightens
>
> one last breath
> and it floats
>
> out of reach
>
> — from *Paper House*

MY MOTHER TOLD ME LATE IN HER LIFE THAT I WAS "an easy child." I think she had forgiven me for the stress I caused her in our wedding planning. Because of schedules, we could only have the ceremony on July 2, 1954, the day before my parents moved from western Kansas to British Columbia. This meant that she hosted wedding guests with much of her household packed up, ready for the travel trailer. And in the reception line, our guests from the church were also saying goodbye to their pastor and wife. Tears and smiles, congratulations and benedictions, all in the same evening.

My parents were relieved to have me married and independent. They sent all eight of us off, one by one, with gifts of bedding, smiles, and confidence. Letters

once a week and an occasional phone call were enough contact. After a honeymoon in the mountains of Colorado, we packed up our new green Ford to begin our wedded life in Chicago, where Louis was a second-year medical student at Northwestern University.

I had lived in Omaha for one year, but Chicago was more challenging. Not only was I learning how to be a wife, I was applying for jobs and trying to navigate by bus and the elevated train. Our apartment was near Forty-Seventh and Woodlawn, an area that had once been elite but was now changing with the departure of residents to the suburbs and the influx of blacks from the South. The former Girls' Finishing School across the street was divided into small rooms for renters where groups of families crowded in.

We began our married life in a third-floor apartment "brownstone," in which the first and second floors were occupied by other medical students and their families. We were just learning to know each other when tragedy struck. The oldest child of the family downstairs, age six, accidentally hung himself on his bunk bed. We heard the mother's screams when she discovered him, helped with the attempts to bring him back with mouth-to-mouth resuscitation, and tried to help carry the family's grief during that first year.

The whole neighborhood was jittery. In our first year the pharmacist at the corner store was murdered. Our tires were slashed, and there was a bullet hole in our front door. I was alert to pickpockets and knives on my bus rides and transfers to the elevated train. My job as secretary at Wesley Memorial Hospital, in the safer near north side of the city, included the releasing of bodies from the morgue to mortuary personnel. I would pull out the long drawer and identify the body by the tag attached to a big toe. In the same room lay a cadaver in autopsy, the brain exposed or the intestines spread over the side while the pathology resident sometimes sat beside the body eating a sandwich. Half the day I spent typing up EKG reports in the cardiology department, and during one lunch hour when I was the one assigned to answer the phone, a patient collapsed during a stress test. The doctors, unable to get a heartbeat, cut his chest open to massage his heart as they shouted to me to run for nurses and emergency equipment. I had married a medical student; I had married a life of trauma.

The domestic rhythms were a different challenge and a kind of solace; I took the role of cook and house-cleaner as expected in those days. As Louis continued his preparation for his chosen work, I was changing my life. Instead of continuing my college education, my main pursuit now was to provide support and care for another person who was achieving his goal. At a time when this arrangement was the norm, the adjustment was continual and challenging for me, even at the young age of twenty. Who was I now?

My mother, naturally impatient, had not taught me how to cook. You'll learn as you do it, she said, washing up the last pots at her magical speed. I was slow and awkward with household work, even as I had done my share of chores at home. Now we wanted to entertain our friends, and I began to learn in huge leaps.

A different kind of trauma was my slow release from a piety that was partly a protection from current culture. Movies, for example. When my new husband finally persuaded me to see a film version of Shakespeare's *A Midsummer Night's Dream* in a theater, we found it as part of a double feature, the first show being George Bernard Shaw's *Major Barbara*. The little theater was filled with University of Chicago students who found the opening scene of a Salvation Army street band hilarious. I had been forced to do street meetings in the college I last attended, and though I had negative feelings, I didn't understand the cynicism of the play. I was offended and wanted to leave. But Louis persuaded me by urging, "Please, let's stay and see how it turns out."

In *Major Barbara*, written in 1905, Shaw was raising issues of justice, wealth, and poverty, and of business and religion, all with a comic edge. Both Shaw and Shakespeare include darkness within the art of comedy. *A Midsummer Night's Dream* exposes the weight of love and marriage, even as it celebrates love's power to mend what can be broken. The forest night is filled with strange and wondrous events and creatures. Amid all that, Shakespeare asks, what does it mean to lose one's individuality in favor of a new identity in the love of another?

The tests of medical school, then residencies, were various. Pasadena, California, offered its wondrous climate and mixed culture of old money and the challenges of the late Fifties. The setting of palm trees, large poinsettia bushes in December, and oranges ripening on our neighbors' trees seemed magical and somehow permissive. The smog and haze hid the nearby mountains for the first weeks, then surprised us one Sunday morning by appearing. Silent, barren mountains, quite near, as if to make a claim on us.

Here I learned about isolation as I waited with our firstborn child for support. Internship, we had been warned, would be exhausting and lonely, and it was. For days and nights in succession I saw no one except my new baby, whom I deeply loved, yet whose cries echoed my own fears and inabilities. I remember with gratitude the silver-haired woman in the grocery store who stopped to admire my beautiful daughter as I bought the least expensive meat available—beef heart for twenty-nine cents a pound.

Back in the upstairs apartment I boiled that heart while the little chartreuse radio played classical music all day. These were the Fifties, with the expectations of home and security, of small waistlines and carefully coifed hair. Mothers stayed home to create and maintain perfection for their husbands and children. While our home for a year was a small upstairs apartment in the house of a widow, I knew that one day I would be challenged to a high standard. In a mother's club where we attended church, I received with gratitude the gift of support and felt great relief in the outbursts of several women who dared to announce that they were breaking the tight rules of housekeeping and mothering, and that it was okay. Theirs was a kind of holy laughter, as they seemed able to accept themselves and to celebrate their limitations.

When we chose California as our place to open a pediatric practice, we knew that we would miss the support of parents and the familiar hometown. We had tasted the beauty of the Pacific Ocean, the grandeur of Yosemite National Park, and the growing culture of this state, and now we were reluctant to leave. Louis remembered the amazing family trip to California at age four, when he visited Catalina Island, the giant Sequoia redwood trees, and his uncles, aunts, and cousins living in the San Joaquin valley. Most importantly, a new children's hospital in Fresno was a magnet for incoming pediatricians. In addition, some of our college friends were completing PhDs and moving to Fresno to be on faculty at Fresno Pacific College.

After fifty years in this city, the marriage has thickened in its accumulation of shared experience. Raising four children here has carried the mix of weight and lightness as we tried to learn how to parent in the midst of the turbulent Sixties and the Cold War atmosphere, and as doors opened to medical discoveries, to women, and to greater awareness of racial and cultural issues.

Our small, innovative church, College Community Mennonite Brethren, was a shelter as well as a place of challenge to live the gospel, the rituals and rhythms of the church year nourishing and comforting us. Our gratitude to God overflows as we watch our children and grandchildren grow and make choices that bless the world. After thirty-seven years of practicing pediatrics in this city, my husband retired with relief, even as he missed his colleagues and patients.

The house in which we have lived for more than forty years has allowed us much space to stretch and to share our lives. After eight years in a two-bedroom house in Old Fig Garden, we began looking for more space. We found a house on Lane Avenue near Fresno Pacific College in another older settlement of the city, a house that seemed to be looking for someone to care for it and use it. Its location has allowed us to offer apartment-living for college and seminary students who have enriched our lives in numerous ways. Our first roomer, Bill Braun, eventually returned to become pastor of our church and remains a dear friend of our family. Among many others who expanded our lives was Rodney Harder, an artist, now in New York City, who allowed us to become part of his own journey of search and discovery in the visual arts, blessing us with his friendship and paintings.

The care of this large house and yard can become heavy at times, but the spaces continue to offer room for hospitality, memory, and the play of light and shadow through the seasons. The Tudor style is rare in this city, its lower level of double-wall brick supporting wood and stucco gables above. The builder, we learned, was given money to replicate his ancestral home in England, which he obviously adjusted, adding a large picture window in the dining room and an entire wall of windows above the kitchen cabinets—providing abundant light and an open view of the gardens. One December day a man rang our doorbell and offered to do electrical repairs. He looked around and said that he had stayed in a house exactly like this one on a choir trip to York, England. After repairing numerous switches and connections, the house now ablaze with Christmas lights, he walked into the foggy night and disappeared.

When we bought the house, Louis began refurbishing the backyard beyond the courtyard garden, which had once been a field of peach trees that were now uprooted. He planted a lawn and developed a garden with a pool and a Japanese bridge. Gradually we planted more trees so that now behind the wisteria and grape arbor we enjoy magnolia, flowering peach, and cherry trees and the summer bloom of crape myrtles. Outside the dining-room window we have a view of a small grove of birch trees, which we planted after our first journey to the Soviet Union in 1975. We bought two Japanese maple trees for a wedding anniversary and planted them just outside the living-room windows, where we see their lacy leaves turn brilliant in autumn. The garden, with its expansion of roots and branches as the seasons unfold, fortifies the joy of staying in one house, as if to say, "Let's stay and see how it turns out."

What "turns out" at this point is that our married journey is the mix of harvest and relinquishment. After some years of home care, Louis is now in a skilled-nursing facility. This house will eventually be someone else's home. The thickness lightens as we rest in the mystery of life itself, those dramatic beginnings enlarging us in ways we could not have imagined.

5

Piano:

Music as Presence

1933 to the Present

FRESNO, CALIFORNIA, AS WE APPROACHED IT ON Highway 99 in July of 1961, was a glare in the eyes, asphalt parking lots, and wrecked cars in heaps baking beside the road. It was dry grass and dust held down by three rusty cars and a motorcycle in front of a two-room house. We were moving here to begin a medical practice, to a city that needed pediatricians; a hub of commerce for ranchers, immigrant laborers, and diverse businesses, we had heard, but which now seemed fragile. We would need to find something strong and sturdy if we were to stay, something that would hold us safely over dry, quaking earth.

Off the highway, however, we found a city laid out in square blocks and shaded streets with manicured lawns. We also found a small, furnished house to rent. One of our first purchases was a used baby grand piano. In this unfamiliar place, it was an oasis for me as I coped with the demands of two preschoolers and the absence of my husband, who put himself on call day and night to get a jump start in his practice. Bach, Debussy, nursery songs, and hymns softened the harsh heat of afternoons, and the curved, simple line of the piano's body was pleasing, even if the surface was cracked with age.

We had moved a piano before. In our first year of marriage we bought an upright that scraped the banisters as it was hoisted up to our third floor flat on the south side of Chicago. I had seen it exposed to the street from my office window, a piano abandoned by evicted tenants, the wrecking ball swinging before it like a metronome. Before the day was over my husband had arranged to buy it for twenty-five dollars and to have it moved for seventy-five more. It was a reckless, loving act, considering that its cost represented nearly half of our month's income.

<hr>

MY LOVE FOR THE INSTRUMENT GREW IN SPITE of early struggle: before my first piano recital at age six, I slammed my finger in the car door. I lost my nerve and memory in school contests, and it was clear that my skills in technique were limited. What ran deep and insistent for me, however, was the pleasure in the harmony, the dissonance and resolve, the way my hands on the keys could make the sounding board resound. Playing the piano was a cooperation with keys and hammers, an invocation of the amazing variations in the sounds of eighty-eight keys, and an assent, it seemed, to keep moving into the glorious cathedral of piano literature as an amateur. After all, the word "amateur" comes from the Latin for "lover."

A piano was present when I was born in a Saskatchewan winter, seventh child in the family, the older siblings taking lessons. In recent years I met a man who remembered my birth. He had been a student in my father's one-room country schoolhouse. It was December and time to rehearse for the annual Christmas program, and he with other students walked to the little teacherage on the schoolyard to practice with the piano. My father announced to the children that there was a new baby in the house, would they like to meet her? First sounds, children singing around the piano, music with body warmth, and then on the program night, being carried under stars as part of the procession behind the piano as it was rolled over snowy boards to the schoolhouse.

By the time I began lessons my parents paid for them by offering the use of our home, in Minnesota then, as a studio one afternoon a week. Mrs. Roberts stepped off the Greyhound every Thursday noon at the end of our graveled street and walked to our house in her dainty boots and fur-trimmed coat. Her cultured, gentle ways carried me into another world, thirty minutes of patient instruction that was sometimes interrupted when she became enraptured with the melody, when her training in singing broke through. Then she would sing the beat in crescendo, her rich contralto melting the frost from our snow-whipped windows.

Year after year the piano stood in our small living room, an imposing presence challenging me to master another key, to drill scales and arpeggios, and to learn my first Mozart sonata. Overriding it all, however, was the possibility that I could play well enough to be one of the honored accompanists for congregational singing in our church. All leadership there was adult and male. The piano and organ accompanists, however, were often female, sometimes teens. We younger girls would lean forward and watch and listen, hopeful for such an honor. My sister and I spent many summer afternoons playing and singing hymns, partly in preparation, but also because they offered comfort in a time when music and language combined to become a source of both challenge and comfort. These were the uncertain years of World War II. "Holy God, we praise thy name" and "Great is thy faithfulness" became a part of my body as our voices and hands created a resonance that grew beyond ourselves.

In Chicago, in our first home after we were married, the piano became a sort of refuge. After typing cardiac reports and EKG evaluations all day, I would join my husband in our apartment where he was memorizing *Gray's Anatomy*. He showed me the heart's chambers, the way the valves work, how sometimes they close up hard as stone. He studied the ear, its delicate coil and drum, the eye's amazing lens. I was taking classes in literature, reading Fitzgerald and Wallace Stevens, their language opening new vistas, then opened the book of Chopin's nocturnes seeking the path of melody and its attendant harmonies, my left hand laboring at the leaps through unexpected passages as the nocturne moved toward a resting place. Both of us learning by means of language, and both of us aware that words were limited, that the amazing body was able to know something large and shimmering, and perhaps devastating, that lay beyond language. Music without words, like Mendelssohn's "Songs Without Words" and other "pure music" compositions, called to me, inviting me to enter and discover that vast reservoir that lies under good literature.

Chicago's gales were meaner than any I had felt in Saskatchewan or Minnesota. They tore through the skyscraper canyons from the lake and pressed me against the hospital wall. These early years of marriage, and that city with its layers of sociological challenges, corruption in the mayor's office, and the restlessness of African Americans in our neighborhood, were dramatic. It was the offering of the arts—the Chicago Art Institute, the Chicago Symphony, and the theater—that became part of our shelter and exploration. We were attending an integrated Mennonite church that nourished our roots of faith. In that church we sang in a choir that performed Bach's "St. John Passion" and heard Jesus' teachings about justice and mercy. During those years in Chicago we learned that art and faith could reside in the same space, that

solutions for our world would require the giving of
ourselves in ways that could be painful but could also
lead to joy and beauty.

Twenty years later in Fresno, after our youngest
child was settled in school, I began giving lessons to
children on our Yamaha conservatory grand piano.
It was a way to share this fine instrument and the
love I held for it. Some students learned to listen to
the wonder of melody and harmony, some mainly
struggled with those black heads with stems dancing
on too many lines. The demand of coordination was a
mountain and the development of technique a never-
ending range. But there it stood, offering itself. Some
would walk in with their sighs and open their books
once again to try to make those notes into something
more, that elusive quality that reverberates at the edge
of all we try to make, whether art or marriage.

During these years I began to test myself in cre-
ative-writing classes at our local university. Back to
language and its power and possibility. I had searched
for good literature to support me in my lonely role as
mother and homemaker and discovered that excellent
writing was important soul food. Gradually the yearning for creating such work myself began to lift its head.
As I found myself engaged in the writing of poems
and in reading many poets, I recognized the obvious
crossover from poetry to music. Here, too, was rhythm
and sound, development of a theme, and a new vista
opening—what all art offers. Just as in learning to play
the piano, or any instrument, one begins with rules,

technique, and practice. Joan Oliver Goldsmith writes how we are "teaching the notes to our muscles, engraving the geography of the music onto our minds; playing with phrasings, dynamics, and tempo," yet how, after mastery, we need to let go so that the music becomes creation with its yearning, awe, and passion. I learned that in writing as in piano playing we continue to seek the "right song" that holds within it some connection to the rest of our lives, and as Goldsmith puts it, "a connection that is struggling towards consciousness."

When my grandchildren come to our home, we often sit together at the piano to sing. This week one chose the book of folk songs from the New York Metropolitan Art Museum, songs illustrated with visual art. He selected "Bringing in the Sheaves," a song I remembered singing in four parts with my church congregation when I was a child, the basses rumbling like threshing machines and the sopranos soaring over them, words and music blending their powers. Before us in the book was Bruegel's golden painting "The Corn Harvest," with the harvesters among thick stands of wheat, some resting and eating together, some working their scythes in solitude. A timeless scene. Seed and planting, the weathers, and then harvest. What we store up for the times of deprivation.

My mother spent the last twenty years of her life in Fresno, "this dusty place," as she described it. We spent the last summer of her life sitting at her bedside singing hymns, helping her at age ninety-five to let go. It was a typically hot California valley summer, the mockingbird holding forth from the magnolia tree outside her door, the mountain snows pouring down their saving flow. "Sing a hymn, any hymn," she would say with dry lips and bright eyes peering out of her bony face, and I would begin—"It is well with my soul" or another. After the opening phrase she chimed in with a strong alto, or a high tenor, as she often had from the kitchen when I was learning to play. One hymn and then another and another.

After her final, monumental breaths, I came home and sat down before that cool row of keys and the sturdy grace of the instrument and played Chopin, letting the sorrows and resolves wash through me. I remembered, then, her sitting near the stove knitting mittens on howling winter nights so long ago, sitting at last after a day of house and family care, calling to me to bring another basket of corncobs to burn. That chore was a repeated irritation, my having to run into the dark, cold shed, the dry cobs scratching my hands as I scooped them into the bushel basket. They burned too quickly. But that heavy stove gradually warmed into a glow that lasted into the night.

6

Pomegranate:
The Ancient and the New

1961 to the present

WE LIVE IN A VALLEY OF BIBLICAL FRUITS. GRAPES, figs, olives, and pomegranates thrive in this subtropical climate. The soil of an ancient seabed, the hot summers, and the irrigation of mountain snows combine into a fertile setting.

In our own garden a lovely, gnarled fig tree spreads its many arms and large, rough leaves. It supplies us and the birds with at least three crops of pale pink succulence every summer. Even our neighborhood fox jumps up for the ripest ones. Our one pomegranate tree offers its sweetness in autumn, the weighty balls of rosy skin clinging to the branches of lacy leaves as the seeds gather sugar until their pouches split, ripening just in time to be placed in honor on our Thanksgiving and Christmas tables.

Our first pomegranates in Fresno arrived as a gift to my pediatrician husband, a shopping-bagful. What to do with these unfamiliar globes?

"Cut them open and suck out the juice," my husband said, as he stood over the sink in a kind of rapture.

Suck and chew and spit out the seeds in primal joy. The children were enthralled while I somewhat carefully let my teeth sink in to release the astringency, this juice that is both sweet and tart. When I discovered that the splattered stains were almost impossible to remove, the new rule in the house was for the children to take off their clothes and sit in the bathtub to eat this strange fruit.

The seeds are bright jewels in a leather-like cup, divided into sections of white parchment. Amazing and ancient. I fell in love, and each year press them for juice to drink and to make jelly. Other times I meticulously remove the seeds for salads. The grandchildren remind me each year to make their favorite Jell-O salad, which features the seeds whole, softened enough in the gel to swallow them. And at Christmas I send home with them a jelly jar of this exotic fruit, each spoonful like a large ruby on bread or waffles.

Fruit of mythology. In the Greek myth of Persephone, the pomegranate is called the fruit of the underworld. Persephone is persuaded to swallow one seed, resulting in the requirement that she return into the dark earth for a part of every year. Pliny offers advice on preserving this fruit by hardening it in sea water, then drying it in the sun for three days. Homer places the tree into his Garden of Alcinous. In the Qur'an it is called the fruit of Paradise.

It is the biblical source that intrigues me most. The tree is mentioned in Haggai, Song of Solomon, Deuteronomy, Numbers, 1 Samuel, and especially Exodus. In Exodus 39:24-26, the part of the instructions for the tabernacle call for pomegranates to be attached to the hem of the priests' robes: "They made pomegranates of blue, purple, and scarlet yarn and finely twisted linen around the hem of the robe. And they made bells of pure gold, and put the bells between the pomegranates all around on the hem of the robe, alternating a bell and a pomegranate all around on the hem of the robe for the service, just as the Lord had commanded Moses." This instruction with its repetitive phrasing sounds like a song or poem, lifting the fruit into textile art, exciting the senses as they shimmer between the ringing golden bells. The High Priest enters the Holy of Holies through the dyed curtains, the fruits of earth crafted into beauty and swinging around his feet.

What has this to do with a Mennonite woman taught to live simply and frugally? My lessons in preservation of fruits and vegetables began when I was tall enough to lean over the kitchen counter to peel and slice, hours at a time. It was tedious, and it was the way of winter survival—corn, peaches, peas, beans, tomatoes, and even chicken. The gleaming jars were carried into the cellar to which my mother's friends were invited to view the harvest behind glass.

Canning changed to freezing when I moved to this valley, and soon fresh produce was available year around. I have the luxury to choose, sometimes slicing luscious peaches for frozen pie fillings, or crushing the figs for jam, and every year I am willing to stand by the sink to patiently remove the seeds and press the halves of pomegranates for juice. Sometimes I experiment with sauces for pork and chicken. And now the fruit is noted as a super-healthy one. Loaded with antioxidants, we now can "drink and live," if we pay.

I have the Jesuit missionaries to thank for bringing the trees to California. With these trees they brought the rule of the Catholic Church. Grace and beauty, but with boundaries. For the Jews the fruit is a symbol of the Torah—an average of 613 seeds in each pomegranate for the 613 commandments. Such numbers remind me of the hours of slicing and peeling, and of the need for preservation.

Litany and liturgy, the daily prayers, what nourishes and saves. But I also think about the knife cutting through when I divide the fruit into halves, 306 and a half commandments in each section, which I crush in my pomegranate squeezer, then pour out the brilliant juice into a cup and drink—one-half for the first commandment of fulfillment: "Thou shalt love the Lord thy God with all thy heart and soul and mind," and the other half for the second, "and thy neighbor as thyself."

7

Entering the Wild:
My Writing Journey

1933 to the Present

Education

IN THE FALL OF 1977 LOUIS AND I TOOK OUR FIRST trip to New England. After medical meetings at Yale University, we drove through the golden woods of Connecticut and Massachusetts, visited the waterfront at Mystic, saw the highlights of Boston, and one day toward dusk drove into the town of Amherst. At this hour the house where Emily Dickinson wrote her seventeen hundred poems was closed to visitors. Standing outside of it was satisfying even then, like her poems, which were so much bigger than this silent house and which lured me into new territory.

My attraction to Emily's poetry began in high school, but not until I returned to college in 1965 to finish my degree did I begin to explore her work. I

chose her as the subjects of several papers; one of
them, "The Religion of Emily Dickinson," sprang
from my fascination with her rejection of the current
expressions of Christianity even as she acknowledged
the Presence in profound ways. Her astringent poems
were magnets, immensities caught in a few lines. Her
close observations of nature could open the universe.
One small woman in white, so different from me. No
husband, no children. She had "stopped being theirs,"
while I had walked the aisle for salvation a number of
times to be sure that I was. No pious language, whereas
I was immersed in it. And yet, I admired that key in her
apron pocket that unlocked a door to new and amazing
language. Her rhythms were like those of the hymns I
sang. Her words were unexpected and sometimes wild.
Nothing about that house explained her, but I was content to breathe outside of it as the darkness grew large:
"Because I could not stop for death..." "I heard a fly
buzz when I died..." "A narrow fellow in the grass..."
"Wild night, wild nights, were I with thee..."

The journey to New England came after we had
made several trips to Europe. Louis and I were grate-
ful for the way that history and art opened to us in
those travels. We also grew in our curiosity about our
heritage in those places, this interest supported locally
by our historian friends and scholars at Fresno Pacific
College and Seminary. And as charter members of a
Mennonite Brethren church, we were reaching back
to the first church in the book of Acts and seeking

illumination in the stories of the Reformation for our development as a congregation. It was a fertile time.

When my husband was in his first years of medical practice in the 1960s, I was a wife and mother at home with three small children. During that socially restless time I looked for stimulating reading, hungering for good literature and thoughtful commentary from Christian writers. I discovered C. S. Lewis and Robert Farrar Capon, among others. I returned to college part-time to finish my bachelor of arts degree when I was in my thirties. At Fresno Pacific College I completed the degree in English, inspired by Wilfred Martens and other young and vibrant teachers fresh out of graduate schools. When I graduated in 1968, Martens encouraged me to become a creative writer, surprising me. I had thought of my degree as personal enrichment and some kind of security should I need to become employed.

After my father died in 1970, I became interested in recording the story of his early life, his immigration as a teenager from Ukraine to Canada, and the story of his family who remained in the Soviet Union. He had written only a few pages of autobiography and rarely spoke about his early experiences. I knew that he had left five siblings in Ukraine when he immigrated as an orphaned teenager to Canada in 1910. In the late 1930s he received his last letters from them, and not until 1956 did he learn from his youngest brother that he was the only sibling to survive the famine and war. His telephone call to me when he received the letter was a sign of his deep yearning. I was determined to learn more.

The novel *The Blue Mountains of China* by Rudy Wiebe, set in Ukraine and Canada and depicting the struggles of Mennonites, was a major inspiration — history and life could be told artistically. He challenged my assumptions about how to write a story by scrambling the linear telling, his characters growing rich with unexpected placement in the action, and by his skill in depicting their complexities. His first book, *Peace Shall Destroy Many*, a major breakthrough in telling of Mennonite immigrants living in Canada's small towns, opened the door for other writers. Wilfred Martens at Fresno Pacific College invited Rudy to a writers' conference, which I attended. It was a strong stimulus for me. He also invited Katie Funk Wiebe, a rare woman's voice in our church journal. Her opinion columns pressed at the borders as she bravely addressed current concerns and issues in the 1960s and '70s.

In 1978 I formed a writers group that met in my home. In the intervening ten years after graduation, I had given birth to our fourth child and was parenting teenagers. After Louis and I made a visit to the Soviet Union in 1975, I had written a short series of poems as a gift to him. On this journey we tasted our history in major cities like Kiev and imagined the life of our grandparents and my father in that area. We also witnessed a number of Jewish doctors meeting their relatives at bus stops. These tearful reunions caused me to long even more to one day meet my cousins who had been exiled to Kazakhstan during the 1940s. My nephew, Stan Jantz, also interested in writing, encouraged me after reading the poems, to host a writers group. Phyllis Martens, a writer who attended the meetings, brought a poet friend with her, Carol Robberson, who suggested that I go to Fresno State University to study with the poet Peter Everwine.

In January of 1980 I registered for an advanced poetry writing class. I was forty-six years old. That spring semester I not only "stood outside the house of Emily Dickinson," I figuratively walked into her bedroom, where she had written and bound her seventeen hundred poems. My domestic life, like hers, was now opening to the unknown, the wilderness that the creative life demands. Everwine offered his high standards for poetry with patience and insight, and by the end of that term I allowed myself to enter language as a way to discovery of self and the world that became a challenging new terrain for me. Everwine stressed the power of image, the music and rhythms of language, and the test: "Does this poem arise out of necessity? Or is it an attempt at art for art's sake?" His own poems were high examples of lyric simplicity and quiet brilliance.

After that semester I chose to enter the master's program in creative writing, which offered me exposure to other excellent teachers, including Philip Levine. His workshops challenged me with his passion for poetry, commitment to excellence, and resistance to pretense. His wit and, at times, irreverence, were directed toward all that was false, and his encouraging comments on my poems were crucial. In Chuck Hanzlicek's literature classes I was exposed to twentieth-century poets, including Theodore Roethke, whose greenhouse poems were emblems of early influences in my own life. In Everwine's literature classes I was introduced to Eastern and South American poets in translation, offering a broader view of the challenges and the struggles of the twentieth century. Eventually I found Sylvia Plath, Anne Sexton, Elizabeth Bishop, and Adrienne Rich, and as I read them, I also needed to confront the suicides of Plath and Sexton. What about writing poetry could lead to death? Was I entering a danger zone? And did I have permission? I realized that "becoming a poet" could lead to divorce, misery, and even suicide.

In our very large home I chose a small room in which to write; in fact, it was built as a butler's pantry off the kitchen with a wood storage box to feed the fireplace on the other side of the wall.

I chose it because of its proximity to the kitchen fireplace and its cozy warmth in our huge, drafty house. And maybe I chose this space because its size allowed me to focus. Or was I subconsciously keeping limits on my new love, fearful of allowing it to overwhelm me or to take me too far away from my expected duties as wife and mother? And what were my first duties?

I was now on my own in a new place, entering a discipline and craft that would absorb my best energies. Our three older children were "out of the nest" in college and professional schools away from Fresno. Only our youngest child remained, and I found the hours to study and write.

I made changes in my relationship to church duties and some social events, reserving time and energy for this new work. The necessity for solitude was sometimes fearful, as I required hours away from domestic duties.

Beginning with my father's story, I found myself moving into the dark woods of his mother's suicide, this secret sorrow that I first learned about the day after his death. I was the only child out of eight who was present at his death; my mother had not understood how quickly he was failing. The morning after he died she climbed into my bed sobbing. I held her, and we cried together. And when she caught her breath, she told me a story I had never heard. Several months before this, my father had asked her whether he had ever told her about his mother's death? He had awakened from a nightmare, shaking. She embraced him, assuring him, yes, before they married he had asked whether his mother's taking of her own life would be a hindrance. She said no, even as some thought that such an act could be an inherited trait. For me, then, his death became a double grief; I mourned the loss of him and the tragic death of my grandmother, plus the sorrow that my father had silently and deeply carried all of his years.

Poems About My Father became part of my master's thesis—his childhood in Ukraine, his immigration to

Saskatchewan, and his life as a schoolteacher and survivor, while four of his siblings died in the famine and war. At the center was a poem in four parts: "These Words Are For You, Grandmother," my effort to give language to the tragedy. I wrote that poem in one of Levine's workshops, where his help and encouragement were vital. At the time I assumed that this secret should not be published, but as I held it in my heart and hands, I gained confidence, which was corroborated by my elderly cousin traveling through. When I asked her about the poem she said, "Well, it's time that someone tells the story."

Because of his historical connections, Paul Toews in the Center for Mennonite Brethren Studies at Pacific College offered to publish these poems in a chapbook. My friend, Rodney Harder, drew symbolic images. The books were first offered for sale at the North American Conference of Mennonite Brethren churches in Reedley, California, in 1984. I was given a small display table in the foyer of the church where the delegates were deliberating the programs of the organization. My fears were overridden by the conviction that the truth should be told and by my growing commitment to the search for what lies hidden.

Family History

I WAS BORN IN 1933, THE YEAR THAT HITLER CAME
to power, the year that he closed the gates of the park
named Dachau. Stalin was imposing the Ukrainian
famine. In the United States Franklin D. Roosevelt
was beginning to develop his New Deal policies, and
prohibition officially ended on the very day I was born.
My parents, living in Canada and teetotalers, might
not have noticed, but much later I read the headlines
of the *Chicago Tribune* given to me as a birthday gift
and saw the photos of Chicagoans opening whiskey
casks in celebration.

The seventh child, I was conceived after my mother
asked her Catholic doctor for birth control advice and
was refused. We lived about thirty miles from Saska-
toon, Saskatchewan, where our house, called a teacherage, stood at the edge of the schoolyard. When my
mother and I visited the place in 1982, we found only
the front, concrete doorsteps and a few bricks from the
foundation remaining in the wheatfield. The summer
of my first year our family moved to a larger school and
teacherage, the Riverbank School. My first memory is
of being rocked at dusk in my sister's arms close to the
wood-burning stove as my mother prepared supper. An
elemental scene.

Born in a Saskatchewan winter, I must have closed
my eyes against the glare reflected by vast stretches of
snow. What remains are the memories of light from

the oil lamp with the whole family sitting around the table as my mother cut her fresh loaves of bread, set the big bowl of borscht, and one day opened the wheel of cheese that came as a gift from the government. I remember how she clapped her hands in amazement and laughed. Not until much later did I learn about the Great Depression. My first "poem" at age six or seven was offered to my family sitting around the table: "Into the snow / the shovels go!" as I held up the spoon and dramatically plunged it into the sugar bowl. Their surprise and laughter felt like approval; I might try that again!

These Saskatchewan years hold mostly carefree memories. Our family played games and sang around the piano. We spoke to each other in both German and English. In church we sang and heard preaching in German, a language familiar to these Mennonite immigrants. School programs were entirely in English; poems, dramas, and songs presented in well-rehearsed manner. At home and in church I was fed the poetry of hymns and scriptures, hearing their cadences in two languages, the beauty of the King James English becoming a part of me.

One persistent memory is the one of my father and brothers carrying huge tubs of snow into the porch and dumping the white mounds into a hole in the floor—the cistern that supplied water for the household. That dark hole under a piece of floor that could be lifted held a kind of mystery and danger; I could fall in and drown. In this porch my infant brother,

Stanley, lay in a small gray coffin in April of 1936, a coffin I remember being carried by my brothers over patches of spring snow. But also in that porch I would sometimes stand watching the older schoolchildren at recess, anticipating my entry into the "house of learning."

In 1939 the family moved to Mountain Lake, Minnesota, a huge transition as we said goodbye to many cousins, uncles and aunts, and friends. My father was making a career change from teaching to pastoring a church. We made the move in June and were welcomed into the home of my mother's cousin where, at our late arrival, we were given bowls of fresh strawberries and cream and soft beds.

Those strawberries were the garden of Eden before I was ushered out under the "sword of the Lord." Kindergarten memories are full of sensory play, but once I entered first grade in the local parochial school, I lived under the shadow of personal responsibility for my soul's salvation, which required perfection in behavior, as I understood it, and fear of burning in hell. Miss Epp would warn us that any sins unconfessed "before Jesus came back" would remain unforgiven, and he could arrive anytime. Her pale face and dark eyes punctuated her hard words, haunting me. Miss Rieger saved me by tipping her teaching toward joy. She smiled at us as if she loved us, would draw the Bible stories in colored chalk on the blackboard, whole armies falling with one swoosh of her eraser—the way I wanted my sins removed. We memorized poems and recited them at school programs, and in this place I wrote my first little book of five poems. My subjects ranged from a description of "Grandpa's Boots" to the "Light of the World." My mother, who discarded anything extraneous in our frequent moves, managed to save that little group of pages tied with yarn, surprising me with it years later.

The 1940s were marked by other clouds—war, threat of draft for my brothers, and revivalist preachers coming through. Even as my siblings were thriving in high school, my oldest brother teaching and helping with rent costs, I was aware that "the shadow of the Almighty" might not shield me from death. Radio reports of the dead and my parents' anxiety about their draft-eligible sons were part of the everyday world. To add to our low family income, my father found employment painting houses in summer. I would watch him high on a ladder, his broad brush covering the peel and rot.

We were now a "public family" in our role as preacher's kids. Piety was at a higher level than in Canada, and scrutiny was constant. Some relief came in the shape of music as we welcomed Mrs. Roberts, the gentle lady who arrived on the Greyhound every Thursday to teach students in our home in exchange for our own lessons. Singing was part of our lives as we washed dishes, harmonizing, and as we prepared trios and quartet music for performance.

This was also a time of friendships and social pleasures, our visits to cousins and parishioners, often on their farms, shaping my sense of the shared table and the season of planting and harvest. The local lake just outside of our small town offered that mysterious blue depth for fishing, swimming, winter skating, and baptisms, a place of both beauty and fear. A place where a nonswimmer like me could drown.

During these years I also witnessed my older brothers and sisters going off to college, one of the reasons my parents gave for the move to Minnesota—we were closer to our church school of higher education. Their absence provided a new space for us younger ones, and a challenge, as our siblings had set high standards in study, good grades, and music performance. But hovering over those years was the war, the announcements of casualties after another ship was torpedoed, and the visits we made to Civilian Public Service camps where conscientious objectors were doing alternate national service.

In 1945 my father moved us to Kansas to finish his bachelor's degree. Right after the war ended, I entered sixth grade in a public school in Hillsboro, where Tabor College is located.

That time became a real immersion in college life, as my father and two siblings were full-time students, and we shared our housing with a dozen men students. This move was the beginning of more moves as my father tested his skills as a school administrator back in the parochial school of my Minnesota childhood, then returned to pastoring in several different churches. These major shifts in my teen years were stretches in friendship and self-development, yet also windows into various cultures within the Mennonite world as I learned to cope in new and unfamiliar settings.

The decade of the 1950s began with completing high school, entering college, and getting married, those crucial choices made in a kind of haze of predictable expectation. For women, postwar optimism translated as a retreat into the home, where we could seek perfection as cooks, mothers, wives, and decorators. Yet in my family, such domestication was challenged by the choices of my siblings. In the late 1940s my older sister and her husband chose to go to war-torn Europe with Mennonite Central Committee, where they spent three years in restoration efforts in East Berlin and Switzerland. One of my brothers and his family went to do missionary work as educators in the Congo. My small high school in western Kansas was isolated, but my adventurous older siblings offered me huge new vistas. Two older brothers became pastors, setting a pattern of family connections to sacred vocations, so that eventually all seven of my siblings were either professionals in church work or married to pastors. I would be the only child who had strayed into the secular world of marriage to a doctor.

During those western Kansas high school years, my brother and his wife were my music instructors. They also hosted my sister-in-law's brother, who came to visit and enchanted me with his good looks, humor, and plans for medical school. Marrying Louis on that western plain opened doors to a future that I could not imagine.

In retrospect, perhaps it was my family's history of singing that connects most directly to my need to write poetry. I was born into a household of song, my six siblings all playing the piano and harmonizing. Surely the voice stretching the sounds of language into song lured me to venture into unknown territory.

Nature

THE LARGE TUDOR HOUSE IN WHICH WE HAVE LIVED for the past forty years was set on a thick concrete slab when it was built in the 1940s. Double-wall bricks and steel window frames do not, however, keep the garden from coming in. California style construction of that time was not tight enough to keep the English ivy and creeping fig from entering and thriving behind curtains before I take notice, and the spaces under the outside doors are large enough for small lizards and crickets to come in and visit. Since we moved in, a hive of honeybees has been thriving in our living-room chimney. Their entrance is high in the second story part of the chimney, but sometimes at night they fly down to the fireplace, drawn to the light of the piano lamp around which they buzz in pitches of B natural, B flat, and B sharp.

When we bought the house in 1970, large deodar cedar trees and tall Italian cypresses stood sentinel in the front yard. Orange trees on the west border of the yard offer their glossy leaves year-round, and when the navels ripen at Christmas I remember that gift from my Midwestern childhood—one precious orange in the sack of goodies. After the navels, the Valencias sweeten in juicy globes for summer picking. Enormous pecan trees shade the backyard, a Hilton for squirrels as the fig and pomegranate trees offer their yearly succulent harvest.

On this one-and-a-third-acre lot, Louis found his joyful reprieve from the pressures of pediatric practice. Pulling off his necktie, he often walked through the house without comment to mow the lawns or to dig another water pond. The back area of the yard, which once was a peach orchard, was now an open field waiting for development. After iris and rose beds were thriving, he added willows, birches, crape myrtles, and a magnolia tree.

Only two houses away flows Fancher Creek, a natural stream that became part of the developed canal system in our city. Along its banks stand magnificent California live oaks, towering eucalyptus, also acacias and willows whose branches drift on the high summer current.

Alongside is a walking trail, a place to join the wildlife—mallards, wood ducks, muskrats. and egrets offering birdcalls and the sound of flow. California gray foxes have followed this creek down from the foothills to explore our neighborhood gardens, feasting on our chickens and figs and raising their young in dens hidden in our fertile soil.

Nature, its proximity, the garden's demands, and the seasonal changes insist on entering my poems. The fragrance of jasmine and roses, and the abundance of foliage and grasses are a lush offering as the garden hardly sleeps, the last leaves of the red maple falling only weeks before the daffodils arrive. Like life, I can only control a small part. Like poetry, nature is an undomesticated partner still surprising me with its caprices, its gifts, withdrawal, and death.

The natural world entered my writing world early—childhood memories of gardens, our own yard, the creek walk, and the wilderness of mountains and ocean beckoning a few hours away. Also, memories of childhood's skies, of thunderstorms and tornadoes, winds of Kansas, as well as summer gardens of mulberries, peas, potatoes, and strawberries. Neighborly talk about crops was common in the homes of my friends and cousins, the threats of frost, drought, and hope for abundance as the harvest neared. Louis' phone conversations with his parents always began with the weather, its effect on the wheat crop being a primary concern.

Louis' keen sense of observation as a scientist and photographer was an impetus toward my own growing awareness, to pay attention, to truly see. As he pointed the camera lens down to the smallest wildflower and then tried the wide-angle capture of the Sierra Nevada,

I also paid closer attention. On our visits to the coast he often parked our car at the edge of the ocean, our children squirming in the back seat, as he tried yet another capture of the sunset, that slippery attempt to capture beauty.

Language as description of nature holds a similar recklessness. What may begin as an ode to a perfect moment collapses into its own necessity, one not predicted. I describe the flight and call of swallows returning to build their mud nests under the bridge over the creek and conclude that "our stories are too big for our bodies." The cricket sings himself to death under the piano. The mountains demand my best words, which are never enough, and the ocean tugs its mysteries away from under my feet. I bring in bouquets of roses in spring, then watch the bushes struggle in the brittle heat of midsummer. The jasmine's sweetness breathes from a large vine that pulls down the redwood beams in the patio. Nature will have its way, buckling and straining what we build and what I say. The spaces between immensity and intimacy are more than can be named in one lifetime. I have only begun.

In a poem entitled "Photographs of the Wild" near the end of my book *Snake in the Parsonage*, I describe some of the wonders of the California landscape, and I end the poem with Emily Dickinson standing on a cliff overlooking the ocean, quoting her line, "Wild nights, wild nights / were I with thee," and continue with "That longing to moor the self to love's chaos. / I lift her words like a glass to the call / of this earth.

I drink to the waterfalls / and the wilderness snows that feed the vine, / and to its fruit, the crushed worlds of sugar and light." Whether she was addressing a longed-for lover, or God as Lover, Emily found her domestic life no barrier to what was immense and wild. She found the writing of poetry as her vehicle to travel far and as a safe reservoir for longings and loss that could overwhelm.

Spirituality

DURING MY GRADUATE STUDIES I VENTURED INTO early Dutch literature, my heritage drawing me there. Among the earliest writers was the mystic and beguine, Hadewijch of Antwerp, who opened new and strange spaces with her language in the thirteenth century. Her poetic writings included instruction to her pupils, and among these was the vision of the "upside-down tree." She pointed to the tree as an emblem of our experience with God—the roots pulled out and raised in reversal, the crown pressed into the earth. I used that image in my first full collection of poems, *The Upside-Down Tree.* In this book I explored my childhood, my Dutch heritage, and my travels to the Soviet Union. In a poem about Mennonite history in Amsterdam, I assigned a meaning to the tree, a symbol of both spiritual and bodily needs lifted toward God. This woman's writings had been preserved, and now, seven hundred years later, I found her images illuminating my imagination.

Interest in the feminine view of spirituality had grown during the 1970s, although I was unaware of this literature when I began to study creative writing in 1980. On my own I found the work of Evelyn Underhill and others, recognizing the natural crossover to poetry, a feminine voice probing deeply. In my first published collection, *Words for the Silence*, I end with the poem "Matryoshka Dolls," a description of the nested dolls that I bought on our journey to the Soviet Union in 1975. I describe the dolls as having fewer smiles and flowers on their aprons as they grow smaller, then comment on the smallest doll: "Don't lose her," I caution at the end of the poem, and at a time when I was just beginning to trust my own voice as authentic.

At the same time there stood on my bedside table a wooden statue of Mary, the mother of Jesus. Replica of an early figure carved in the Philippines, this Mary had no arms. She became an emblem of the invitation to repeatedly release myself from the anxious need to shape the choices of my growing children. She also represented an attitude of release about my own writing, to acknowledge that any tendency to manipulations of subject or style in the writing of poems could be a block in the way of discovery.

During this time I attended a national conference of church women that occurred here in Fresno. The Evangelical Christian Women's Conference brought leading feminist theologians to our city. The lectures, discussions, and presentations fed me in ways I had not earlier imagined. When at the concluding meeting we received communion served only by women, I began to weep. Never before had I experienced the Table as the place where women presided and from which they invited me to participate.

My own church home stood out among all other churches in the U.S. Conference of Mennonite Brethren by hiring a woman assistant pastor. While we were not allowed by conference rules to hire a woman as lead pastor, we were thriving under the leadership of a woman. In this church I had my gifts acknowledged in leadership as part of various commissions and the church council, positions in which I grew and learned along the way. During these years I also was invited to sit on the boards of Fresno Pacific University and its seminary, where I raised my voice on behalf of women and artists, and the importance of peace and justice as basic Christian teachings. These opportunities enriched me and added confidence for the task of writing. Perhaps my voice could be trusted.

For me, poetry and spirituality are closely bound. My life experience and deep interest in the Christian journey has persuaded me to agree with Marcus Borg when he writes, "Belief of mind does not transform." Something deeper than information, spoken creed, or rational agreement is necessary. The power of image and metaphor continues to call to me as I read the scriptures and create a new poem. Over and over I am invited and required to enter the unknown dark, the call of memory and experience, the place where mystery lives.

Mennonite teachings stress the importance of servanthood, something that comes rather naturally to women. Or perhaps the generations of women before me have marked my genes.

During the time I began writing I had repeated dreams about large groups of people waiting for me to feed them. Sometimes all I had were two pork chops in the freezer. I knew that I couldn't multiply them as Jesus did, and so I woke up in panic. Sometimes I had left my baby in the crib and traveled to Europe, suddenly remembering him as I was partying. In another dream a train unloaded travelers at our front door, all walking in to have dinner. My self-analysis concluded that either I felt guilty for doing less entertaining, or I was called to feed others with my writing. In either case I was overwhelmed, and gradually I learned to rest in the hope that the poems could nourish others.

Not surprisingly the writing moved me into vocabulary with which I dared to offer unfamiliar language for the holy and for theology. (I had not heard about "theopoetics" until a minister suggested that that is what I was doing.) Certainly the Bible knowledge I have gained in my life and the nurture I have been given in the church continue to be an ongoing stream of sources for writing. Further study and spiritual practice has only deepened that flow. And I continue to be convinced that the Gospels, especially, call me into untried places as I allow the narrative and teachings to become a part of me.

While Hadewijch was the first mystic I encountered, I eventually learned to know some of the writings of more "women in the wild." In 1991, when I was invited by the committee for a new Mennonite hymnal to write new texts using images from the writings of three medieval women mystics—Julian of Norwich, Hildegard of Bingen, and Mechtild of Magdeburg—I was drawn into their fresh images and passion. Their claims of joy and knowledge were written in ways that were beginning to feed the hunger of both men and women in the late twentieth century. My interest in Hadewijch in the 1980s was a preview of these women, but I hadn't imagined anyone singing her words in worship. Now we were in the early 1990s, and these texts were gaining readers, the search for a feminine perspective at last becoming stronger and more acceptable.

The musical setting for one of these hymn texts was by Alice Parker, the well-known composer and arranger, who also incorporated my poems about Mennonite singing into an oratorio. "That Sturdy Vine" was performed by the Jon Washburn Singers and the Vancouver Symphony Orchestra in 1993 and has had subsequent performances in Canada and the United States.

The Mennonite community of writers has been an important source for growth and encouragement. When I was invited to read poetry at a Mennonite

World Conference assembly in Winnipeg in 1990, I met another writer from the United States, Jeff Gundy, who was also invited to read. Each of us knew only one other writer of Mennonite heritage who was seriously studying writing and publishing, while the Canadians were blossoming with writers. Since that year the interest and work has grown significantly. Mennonite colleges and other universities are offering writing courses, and Mennonite writing conferences are attended by two or three hundred people.

This community of writers is a continuing source of encouragement and support, especially my friendship with Jeff Gundy and Julia Spicher Kasdorf.

The two universities in which I have taught poetry, Eastern Mennonite and Fresno Pacific, allowed me to grow as a teacher and a poet. My first small collection published by the Center for Mennonite Brethren Studies was noted by Merle and Phyllis Good, who included me in the anthology, *Three Mennonite Poets*, a real first in Mennonites publishing poetry. Through their publishing house, Good Books, they continue to publish volumes of my collected poems.

The Fresno community of poets, based in the California State University of Fresno, continues to be a sustaining group of friends. A poetry reading series organized by Chuck Moulton brought opportunities for locals to be heard in the Wild Blue Yonder Café. When that series moved to the Fresno Art Museum auditorium, we were enriched by the readings of nationally known poets as well as our own writers. This series, organized by poet Chuck Hanzlicek, was an extension of informal social gatherings of Fresno poets that include our beloved teachers.

When Roberta Spear, friend and poet, returned to this valley to live, she invited me to be a "first reader," one who responds to a poem in progress. A gifted, prize-winning poet, she became a radiant example and support. Roberta's gifts were tested as she combined mothering and supporting her husband in a beginning medical practice, and in that familiar mix, she and I bonded with our writing. Her fine ear and keen sense of the poem were gifts beyond measure. And her poems, often set in this valley where she was born and raised, offered a spirituality as she portrayed her neighbors, family, and laborers with dignity and sympathy. Her early death became another lesson of spiritual strength as she battled leukemia with shining courage.

Emily Dickinson set the example for the spiritual in poetry with her "double vision." When I read her, I am lured into her gift of describing immensity and intimacy, both of which hold a sense of what is wild and not domesticated. I think of the Gospel of John and the "farewell discourses" in the last chapters, where the story of Jesus in conversation with his disciples embraces both great distances and great closeness. The span is huge and it is life.

I am invited to be rooted in love, like the grapevine that drinks from the soil, even rock. "No one can take away your joy," Jesus announces to his bewildered followers. "I am the Vine, you are the branches" is an invitation to receive sustenance and productivity. In those final words before his death, Jesus comforted them with the image that life after death is like a house with many rooms.

Emily writes, "The Infinite a sudden guest / Has been assumed to be— / But how can that Stupendous come / Which never went away?"

In my last collection of poems, *Paper House*, I tried again to find language for the "Infinite," the "Stupendous." My days continue in my domestic setting of home and daily visits to my husband in a nursing home. Could it be that the poem itself is akin to the domestic with its routines and attempts at order? The day opens, the day ends, a rhythm that offers renewal. Even in the wild the sun sets and slows the thaw of winter snow, a kind of measure—like the end of the line or stanza before it turns into the next line—so that the vine is fed and the grape swells into ripeness for harvest and fermentation. So that at last we may sip "the crushed worlds of sugar and light."

8

The Fire, the Light:
A Visit to the Place of My Mennonite Origins

1996

I HAD COME TO SEE TULIP FIELDS, THE PAINTINGS of Vermeer, and the landscape. I had left my little study crowded with books to taste the air of Holland and to smell the light. Our first stop, Haarlem, our small hotel opening out to the Grote Markt, the old city center with its great cathedral, gabled commercial houses, and a statue dominating the center. It is Laurens Janszoon Coster, the Dutch inventor of moveable type, even before Gutenberg, the locals say.

And a half block from this Markt, the oldest Mennonite church still used for services, a stately seventeenth-century meeting place hidden behind rows of houses. We stand in this historic space and in the Jorian Simons room, named for the Haarlem bookseller who burned to death on that Grote Markt, so near to where we had peacefully slept and eaten bread. Before the tulips, before the green fields, these words, books, fire. I had stepped into my history.

Jan Luyken's etching in the *Martyrs Mirror* shows two others burning with Simons. The precious books are flaring and smoking in a huge pile, and in the foreground some men are rescuing the books and throwing them out to the watching crowd. It was 1557, and Menno Simons was writing some of his last pages in Lubeck, his heart on fire.

We drive north to Friesland and trace the paths, lush May washing thick green fields, poplars standing sentinel along every lane, and that almost eerie light through new leaves, even after ten p.m. Light of reason, light of the Word, light on the blood of the martyr, Snijder, which pierced Menno's darkness. And it is the light of vastness, as the huge sky bounces off the North Sea and writes its own news day after day—that we are part of a mystery much larger than any one person or people. Yet its vastness illuminates each detail in the landscape—the one lamb, straws in the thatched roof, the single brick holding up a wall among the others. Light leaves its pearl sheen on the canals of Dokkum where Boniface, first Christian missionary to this region, was murdered by my ancestors. It spreads its rays over churches on the *terpen*, those mud hills created by early tribes, where they huddled to keep from drowning, where their voices chanted over the water, moaning for the light.

Vermeer caught it in the corner of a room, window open, in the poured milk, and in the maid's face. It is the light of giving oneself away, the Christ-light that Menno found. It is the light of knowing we are loved, that we are invited to choose that way of love, that we are to love even those who kill us.

The bulb fields respond, lifting their tongues of fire. Tulips roll out their colors, hyacinths and daffodils pour their perfumes, fields my ancestors fled to save their lives, to save those words that Menno wrote, words that gather and flow into this year, 1996, the five-hundredth anniversary of his birth. These words that I find again, the book burning in my hand.

9

Three Women
and the Pearl

ACCORDING TO THE ACCOUNT IN ROBERT K. MASSIE'S 1967 book *Nicholas and Alexandra: The Classic Account of the Fall of the Romanov Dynasty*, one pearl was found among the bone splinters and ashes after the murder and burning of the last royal family of Russia. The family's tutor recognized it as belonging to the Czarina, the earring "she always wore." The horror of this family's ending is only one of many million atrocities committed for the sake of ideology in the twentieth century, yet I see it connected to my own family's history and experience in that country around the turn of the century.

I think of three women when I read this story: Czarina Alexandra, who chose to hold fast to the power of monarchy, her devotion to family, and her understanding of God's will; Anna Akhmatova, the poet, who chose to stay in her country with her people through

the anguishing years of the revolution and its after-
math; and my grandmother, Helena Wiebe, who lived
with few choices, then chose to take her own life in
an act of desperation. Because the lives of these three
women in Russia overlapped in time and circumstance,
I became interested in exploring their lives in the light
of "the pearl of great price."

The story of Alexandra's pearl was the beginning
inspiration of my poem "Finding the Pearl." I say that
"her hand swerves the path of our century," as she per-
suades the Czar to make decisions that allowed ruptures
in government, a space for the revolution to begin and
flourish. The poem waited unfinished for about a year,
the first stanza dangling in its own space, asking the question, so what? What illumination might be found here?
I unexpectedly found a hinge into the next part after I
looked at Vermeer's paintings of women once again, their
pearls gleaming on their ears and in their hands.

FINDING THE PEARL

They burned the body parts for days,
pouring acid on the stubborn bones, dropping
the ashes into a mine shaft. Even then,
the old tutor, weeping, found evidence,
the Czarina's pearl earring,
one of a pair she always wore.

In 1916 her hand swerves the path of our century
as she writes her letters — the Czar fires
one statesman after another while their son
writhes in his bed, the blood spreading undetected.
Pearl in the tutor's hand,
the nacre which hardened into layers
of death, the sky of Siberia iridescent
over the vast fields of bones.
And the fire in the pit still burns.

I think of her when I see Vermeer's women
in the daylight of their rooms, pearls gleaming
on their ears and held in their hands.
After a lifetime of painting, his brush
made their faces more luminous,
the layers of years building into
such light. Like the pearl of great price —
you sell everything to get it, the Gospel says,
then hold it loose in your hand.
Not the clutching loves of nation, child
or even God, but a beauty that gives itself away.
You walk the museum galleries gazing
at the treasures, then turn another corner
and there it is, the face you didn't know
you were looking for, open as light,
its fires and its tides.

The question remains: how do you hold the precious pearl loosely in your hand? What sort of devotion does not clutch, but gives itself away, like beauty? This question was aroused by a sermon given by a friend and scholar who reminded us one Lenten season that we cannot possess Christ; his life is not something we own and control.

My grandmother's life intersects with Anna and Alexandra as one of three women among the millions who dealt with difficulties and unrest in the early twentieth century in Russia. She was a devoted wife and mother without any particular power or notice, yet by her action and her inability to endure, she became the very source of my existence. A bitter irony. A twist in the history of victims and heroes. How might I see her with Anna and Alexandra as participants in the quest for life and love?

In 1894, the year of my father's birth, Russia was ruled from St. Petersburg by the powerful Czar Alexander III. His dominions were vast and his rule was severe. This Czar's father had emancipated the serfs, yet the peasants were still poor and taxed, and many of the social advances had been reversed. While the palaces and Orthodox churches were glittering with gold and icons, the peasants were taught that suffering was good. "As God wills," the Russian told himself.

Also in 1894, the Czar died, and in his place, son Nicholas, 21, newly married to Alix, a German princess, became the new royal couple. Alix, a granddaughter of Queen Victoria, had much to learn in the new court as she converted from Lutheranism to Orthodoxy and the Russian way of life. In this time of mourning, she soon became a chief support and council to Nicholas. After her children were born, she was also devoted to their care, willing to miss some of the pomp and ceremony, and choosing simpler ways to live. Meanwhile, the world was changing.

During the last years of the nineteenth century, Lenin was smuggling Marxist literature into Russia and joining with others to organize a movement. By 1905, the year of the Bloody Sunday massacre, a general strike had paralyzed Russia. Trotsky became a leader. Workers peacefully marching toward the palace were shot down by the military. During World War I Alexandra became more entrenched in guarding the monarchy and persuaded Nicholas to dismiss statesmen who attempted to initiate a representative government. The birth of her son after four daughters only increased her hope for the monarchy to continue as the will of God. This son was to be the next heir, and when he was found to have hemophilia, her desperate tactics and faith in the wild Rasputin as spiritual guide resulted in deeper entrenchment.

ANNA AKHMATOVA, DAUGHTER OF A NAVAL ENGI-neer, was born in 1889 and raised in Tsarskoye Selo, the Czar's village outside of St. Petersburg. She began writing poems at age ten, after a serious illness. The innocent world of her childhood ended suddenly in 1905 when she learned of the destruction of the entire Russian fleet by the Japanese. It was a shock that lasted her lifetime, she said, this senseless act. That year, along with Bloody Sunday, her parents separated and money became scarce. Anna, however, continued to write, and in 1914 she published her first collection of poetry, a book of love poems. After she married Nicko-lay Gumilyov, the couple became part of a new school of poets called Acmeists, a reaction to French Symbol-ism. Acmeists demanded a return to earth, a deeper understanding of European culture, and a "conviction that God can be found through the here and now on earth, that life is a blessing to be lived." While these theories would be severely tested, her lifetime of writ-ing remained connected to her real-life experience and to the basics of this movement.

Her biographer, Amanda Haight, writes that "early she found her necessity to be a passive instrument dependent on the grace of God, the Word, the living link between heaven and earth." Later, with much struggle and devotion, she identified with the suffering of her people during the years of war and famine. She chose to stay in Russia, unlike most writers, memoriz-ing her poems, then destroying them when her writing became considered criminal activity. Her husband was executed and her son was held for years in prison. As a preface to her moving poem "Requiem," she writes of standing in line for hours day after day in hope of see-ing her son. Another woman recognizes her and asks,

"Can you describe this?" And so she did. As the poem progresses, she traces the suffering of Jesus' mother, Mary, at the foot of the cross as transformation. She would participate in that transfiguration, and as a faithful witness, she could be part of the healing for herself and her country. To be silent would become a crime against humanity. Her devotion and faithful witness was a gift to her people and the world. She died in 1966, a hero of survival and contribution.

Helena Wiebe, my grandmother, was born in 1864 in the Chortitza region of Ukraine, the first settlement of Mennonites from Poland around 1800. I have only one photograph of her as part of a family portrait taken around 1902. The only stories I know are the few that my father told me and that his brother Peter wrote down in his mid-life. I learned about her suicide only the day after my father died, a secret that he bore in sorrow and shame. I then mourned a double loss. In our hallway now hangs an amazing life-size portrait of the family painted by our son-in-law as an interpretation of the photograph, a reminder of both tragedy and survival.

Because farmland became scarce in the Molotschna region of Ukraine, where many Mennonites had settled, my grandfather moved his growing family several times, seeking to lease more fertile soil. Grandfather was not a willing farmer; he preferred doing woodwork, such as making wagons for his children and carving guitars and violins that he played and shared with his wife. In his writings, Uncle Peter acknowledged considerable friction in the marriage, grandmother wanting successful farming and grandfather preferring to make beautiful things. She also spent many months nursing her husband in his fatal illness, during which time he was seeking to invent cures.

There were, however, happy domestic scenes—the joy of parents dressing their little ones in new shoes that their father had cobbled and striped stockings that their mother knitted. They celebrated Christmas with a tree and decorations and the traditional filling of plates on Christmas Eve—by their father, not Santa. The writings describe church services, my aunt singing solos, and my grandfather doing some lay preaching. My father in his brief descriptions remembered climbing the chalk hills near his village. He would go up higher and higher, then look down on the little houses, wondering if his mother was looking for him.

After Grandfather died, my grandmother became poorer and increasingly despondent. The church elders brought food and clothes, but she was unable to bear her loss and in 1908 hung herself in the barn. Rumor has it that my father found the body.

What possible treasure, like the pearl, is recognizable in these three women's stories? What sort of light can be found? Other than difficulty and tragedy, are there commonalities? Surely these three women are separate portraits, like Vermeer's women who turn to us in shadowed rooms, their silent gaze calling to us. I cannot compare the difficult circumstances of each woman, nor can I judge their responses a century later.

All three women made choices that resulted in various endings, and all were subject to circumstances beyond their control. Rather than comparison, I venture some observations.

Alexandra was caught in a time that was testing centuries of tradition, power, and religion bound together. I see her devotion to God, country, and family as admirable but inherently tending toward idolatry. To the end she clutches, even as she prays, sewing the royal jewels into the bodices of her daughters' dresses before the murders. Certainly Alexandra's devotion, like any mother's, was distorted by her fear of loss, especially of her son, a mother's supreme sacrifice. She held the pearl tightly, one could say, the way she understood her role. To hold loosely would have resulted in chaos. Yet I imagine the possibilities of a representative government that might have resisted totalitarianism and the rule of Stalin, that could have saved my uncles and aunts from starvation and death and perhaps even saved her own life and the lives of her husband and children.

As the tragic events unfolded, Anna Akhmatova recognized the need for change in her country. What was false should fall—any system, whether monarchy or communism, that fails to bring some level of freedom and nurture to people. She longed for integrity and compassion in leadership. Although she suffered severe losses, she was blessed with long life and time, at the last, to offer her gifts. After her son was released from prison, she found that they could not live together for long. She had several lovers during her life; she was not the ideal wife or mother. Yet her poems and friendships offered hope and dignity to her people in such a crucial time.

Reflecting on her life, her understanding of the pearl may not be a strict morality but generosity, compassion, and justice. Her open spirit and her poems became part of the healing and strength of many people during the grim years of totalitarian rule, then, later, for others like me who mourned losses, trying to find language for tragedy in my own family.

I don't know if my grandmother held her family tightly. I have learned that she committed suicide after my uncle Peter decided to immigrate to Canada. Her eldest son was forsaking her, she may have thought, leaving her with my father, who was fourteen, and his brother, fifteen, plus four little ones. After her death, Peter would send for these brothers, arranging for farmers in Saskatchewan to pay the ship fare, which they would repay with farm labor.

Did she throw the pearl away with her decision to take her own life? Surely she would not have taken Jesus' words to "lose your life to gain life" as permission. Yet, in essence, she saved the life of my father. Her three daughters would all die in the Stalinist famine, and the baby boys grew up to be young men with families thrust into the Second World War, only the youngest surviving to write my father a letter in 1956.

Three women and the pearl. Piety, devotion, creativity, and the limits of human endurance. "A beauty that gives itself away," I say in the poem. The "nacre which hardened into layers / of death, the sky of Siberia iridescent / over the vast fields of bones" remains, but the glow of those who suffered survives in the living who remember them. The parable of the pearl of great price claims that the kingdom of heaven is the loveliest thing in the world. It is more beautiful than other pearls and requires selling everything else to buy it. In the context of the Sermon on the Mount, I think of the Beatitudes as the layers of nacre, the iridescence offered by those unexpected sources of bliss—the "blesseds" of mourning and humility, mercy, peacemaking, and persecution. All three of these women were caught in the calamities of earthly kingdoms. In remembering them, perhaps I am called to respond to their choices with these very layers. In acknowledging their intertwining lives, I am invited to rest in the mystery of my own existence. My grandmother's face comes alive in the hallway portrait, and I find myself reaching up to stroke her cheek.

For eighty years, no one in my family had been in direct contact with my father's family. I traveled in 1989 to Karaganda, Kazakhstan, to which my Uncle Willie's family had been exiled, and entered the lives of my cousins, survivors of the terrors. When we arrived at their home, a daughter gave me a bouquet of daisies, and after hugs and greetings, we sat down at their request to sing together the ancient hymn, "Holy God, We Praise Thy Name." Its last verse translated into English is: "Holy Father, holy Son, holy Spirit, three we name thee, though in essence only one, undivided God we claim thee, and adoring bend the knee, while we own the mystery." Then we sang the folk hymn "*Gott ist die Liebe*," a song we had sung in our separate childhoods in separate and distant countries. A visiting cousin from Siberia wept as we sang, remembering his survival as street child and orphan.

The nacre flows over an irritant in a cold, chaotic ocean and slowly becomes a thing of beauty. My father crosses that ocean alone at age fifteen and washes up on the shores of Canada. Several years later my mother sees his face in the church choir, "the face you didn't know / you were looking for, open as light, / its fires and its tides."

10

My Father's Ache:
A Restoration of Family

1910 to 1989

DON'T GO

Cousins meet at last after
decades of exile and silence.
I am asked, what compelled you
to seek us out after all these years?

My father's ache, I say.
Like Joseph "his bowels did yearn
after his brother." I have never
seen my father cry except

in the pulpit when he tells
of little Daniel and Willie clinging
to his legs. Don't go, they cried,
as he pried himself loose and sprinted

to hide behind the barn, their wails
echoing, Heinrich, Heinrich, across
the Atlantic and over the plains
where he leans over the Holy Book

and into my yearning for him,
child of his ache for the other–
the self released to run to
the waiting one and be held.

I AM STEPPING OUT OF A BUS IN FRONT OF AN Intourist hotel in Karaganda, Kazakhstan. It is July, 1989, and Louis and I have flown from Moscow with a group of Mennonites exploring our history. The welcoming group stands on the concrete steps of the hotel searching the faces of those exiting the bus, hoping a cousin or uncle has come to hear their stories, maybe to help them. And there he is, my cousin Heinrich, with his wife and two youngest children. I recognize his face from a family photo. His short letter in German said, yes, please come. We will welcome you.

We had ventured into the Soviet Union once before, in November 1975, flying Aeroflot from Los Angeles with doctors and spouses from California. In that Cold War atmosphere we gathered courage to see the country that my father had once claimed as home and from where some of our grandparents had emigrated. I knew that my cousins would have to travel a thousand miles to meet us in a hotel arranged by Intourist, and I did not have the courage to make contact in 1975. When we witnessed tearful meetings of Jewish doctors and their relatives, I regretted my hesitancy. Now, fourteen years later, I was ready.

Would we be able to understand each other? I had practiced the Dutch dialect known as Low German, the language we were assured would be our best communication, testing it with my mother, who, at ninety, kept slipping into English asking, why are we doing this? For Dad, I would tell her. And here we were embracing a young couple with a child in their arms and another running around. "*Eck sie Heinrich Wiebe*," the man announced, "*und dit es miene Fruh, Valya.*" (I am Henry Wiebe, and this is my wife, Valya.) Gentle, handsome, named after my father, he is holding Baby Heinrich. I swallowed hard to keep from sobbing, then tearfully laughed at my broken speech. We understood each other. The words continued to pour out, like a small version of Pentecost, I thought later.

My father had said his last goodbye in 1909 to Willie, the youngest brother, this man's grandfather. Eighty years later, I was the first of our family to greet my father's grandnephew, and soon, his nephew, Willie. We had flown from Moscow over the barren steppes of this place of exile, over the railroad tracks where Aunt Margaret and her children were pushed off cattle cars, stories we would hear in the privacy of their homes. It was the era of Gorbachev and *glasnost*. The Iron Curtain would fall, and most of my cousins would immigrate to Germany.

My father had begun his journey to Canada in the company of his brother Jacob and his oldest brother's family of in-laws. Because of glaucoma the two boys, ages fifteen and sixteen, were left behind in Liverpool, England, where they received medical care and exams. He told about the room they were able to rent, but when they ran out of money, they stood in "soup lines" with an English family who, in pity, claimed them. The boys promised each other that whoever first received an okay from the doctor should journey on alone. My father spoke of this trip across the Atlantic as one filled with hope and excitement. He never was seasick and often stood on deck to enjoy the wind and salt spray. Then the train ride from Quebec, and he stepped off in the little town of Dalmeny, Saskatchewan, that May morning and asked for his brother. He was directed to a field several miles away, where Peter, who was plowing, saw this boy in Russian clothes approach him, then ran to embrace him.

We had flown into Karaganda, but the train stories dominated. The ones in the Ukraine that carried the fathers away to war camps, the ones that took the women and children to the steppes.

The government officials asked Kazakh people to pick up the exiles and put them to work feeding and herding animals, sometimes offering shelter, but more often they had to dig their own mud shelters. In Cousin Willie's home the stories poured out, the ones his father could not put into letters, how mother caught rats in the cow barn and brought them home for supper, hiding them under her skirt. Because my aunt's sister was jailed for gleaning in a field, her children lived with them, adding hungry mouths. They carefully watched her divide the small, cooked portions. "She was always fair," they said tearfully. And when darkness fell and they had no lamp, their mother sang hymns to them, her voice like a rope to which they clung. "*Gott ist die Liebe*," "When I'm lonely and defenseless," her sweet voice releasing "*Heilig, Heilig*," Schubert's soaring melody in the crowded hut, the winter wind howling through the cracks.

What should I do with these stories with which they entrusted me? How should I hold them? What kind of vessel holds pain with respect? I had been driven to seek them by my father's ache and longing, and in return I was entrusted with the litany of their sufferings, their voices, and their survival.

Cousin Willie met us at the hotel in Frunze, Kirghizia, south of Kazakhstan, where he now lived. In front of the hotel he stood with his family wearing a three-piece suit and hat. I announced to my friends in the bus, there is my father! Son of little Willie, the orphaned, clinging boy, his education interrupted by war in second grade, he was employed by the coal mines, as his father had been. But he was also a soloist and choir director in his church. And there was his sister Lena, who was sent to Archangel, Siberia, as a teen to pull logs out of the icy harbor, then forced to pull wagons in the coal mine, "like a pony," they said.

Intourist allows a visit in their home, to their surprise. The world is softening. We eat watermelon and zwieback, the double buns of our Dutch ancestry, tasting exactly like my mother's. We sing and laugh and wipe tears in the wonder of this meeting. Our son, Peter, just graduated from high school, takes videos and waits for translations. The children cling to him, this blond cousin from America. I demonstrate my two phrases of Russian: *spasiba* (thank you) and *da svedanya* (goodbye), and they roar with laughter. We have brought photos of our families, their uncles Jake and Peter, Aunt Katherine, and their families in Canada, also the photos my father received from their parents before the war. The stories continue. We take out maps, we sing another hymn. Bare survival—Uncle Willie beaten, then thrown into a morgue, but he is still alive. Someone walks in and he raises his hand, that hand that said "I am alive," and he was given permission to walk home. I tell them my father's story of saying goodbye, and Lena offers, softly, "Oh, that is a story we also heard." The broken circle is mending.

In 1966 when we took our first trip to Europe, a tour that was to include a flight into Moscow for a few days, my father was excited about writing his brother to meet us there. "I know he would travel all that way to meet you," he told us. When that part of the tour was cancelled, he was disappointed. In his last years my father lived close to his sister for the first time in his life, and he visited her almost daily. During our visit to their home in British Columbia, he arranged for me and my family to visit Aunt Katherine, my first contact with her. She brought out the photo of the family that I had never seen. I gazed in awe, seeing an image of my grandparents and their children, as my own children stood around me.

The stories continue—Uncle Daniel, a trained veterinarian who becomes ill in the "Trud Army" camp. He is thrown off a train alive, and then his wife walks railroad tracks for the rest of her life, looking for him until she is hit by a train and dies. Abram, one of their children, survives, and comes to meet us in his cousin's home. My three aunts starve to death in the Stalinist famine.

The stories find their way into poems, questions of home, and who is my brother. We leave our families to marry an "other." I exist as one born out of the "ache for the other," this gift from God, the Other, that moves us out of self toward the good of another. I carry my father's yearning and so am linked in the mix of his journey.

I recognize this ache in my everyday life and in my study of literature as the best authors "speak what they feel, and not what they ought to say." Shakespeare asks his audience to see life as both tragic and comic at once. In *King Lear*, written near the end of his life, he invites us to feel along with him that this constant mix is what makes life rich and terrible and beautiful. The tragedies threaten to overwhelm us, yet, as Frederick Buechner writes, "in every scene of great suffering, he has someone enter from the wings to relieve it ... and the last word, like Albany's, is a word of mercy."

In the early morning of our departure, my cousins Willie and Abram came to the city to see us off. Willie told me that he hadn't slept well because he was excited by this contact.

"I felt like Simeon," he said, "who proclaimed that 'he had seen the salvation of the Lord.'"

I knew that Willie didn't expect me to rescue him, but in the events of the following two years, he was able to move to Germany with all his children and begin a new life for them. We have embraced them in their new home, and a few of them have found their way to ours in joyful meetings. Abram continues to live in Siberia with his wife and two married daughters. Somewhere in the Urals the bones of Daniel are washed into a ravine or river. Uncle Willie's and Aunt Margaret's graves lie in the crowded cemetery by the Orthodox church outside of Karaganda, the only cemetery allowed for burial. We visited a Wednesday-morning service in that church, the priest in full regalia, a small choir singing the story of the incarnation, incense rising.

When we returned to the car, cousin Heinrich, a Baptist/Mennonite said, "Well, when it comes down to it, we believe in the same story."

This story of yearning for the other and the Other and to be held.

11

Three Women and the Lost Coin:

How Three Women Found Me

1991

IN THE YEAR 1990, THE HYMNAL COMMITTEE OF the Mennonite Church was approaching preparing a new hymnal with the Church of the Brethren. The planners had chosen more than six hundred hymns to nourish their congregations for the coming twenty years or more. Much had changed since the publication of the *Mennonite Hymnal* in 1969.

In that year I was in my late fifties and just beginning to teach poetry writing in several universities. I had earned a master's in English and creative writing, and I had published several collections of poems.

The hymnal committee began looking for texts honoring feminine characteristics of God. Finding none, they sent chunks of writings of Christian medieval women mystics to four or five poets in hope that the images and concepts of those writings might inspire a text. I was sent samples of work by Julian of Norwich, born in 1342, Hildegard von Bingen, born in 1098, and Mechtild of Magdeburg, born in 1207. These three women inspired me to create texts that were ultimately set to music and included in the hymnal. To my amazement, they have since appeared in numerous hymnals, and some have even been translated into other languages.

Even though I was not raised in the church liturgy that might have honored some of these mystic women, I was familiar with hymns and scriptures that had prepared me to consider these images and visions as gifts. My experience with hymns and gospel songs included only a few women writers, such as Fanny Crosby, who rose in popularity at a time of evangelical fervor. These mystics, however, were of another sort. They carried me into new places, their imaginative writings holding claims of joy and knowledge that challenged my perceptions. What did their writings have to do with me, a mature women in the 1990s, near the end of a century when my own children were raising children? What enlightenment might they offer even as we entered the Middle East with our military force in Desert Storm, when AIDS and famine threatened huge populations. Could we really think of God as a mother God, as our

Lover who dances with us, as a Healer who "flies above, below, and through the world" with "lustrous wings"?

As I immersed myself in the poems and prose of these three women, I found myself engaged in the possibilities of devotion and celebration that opened windows in my own imagination.

Could we in the Mennonite church allow this medieval, yet fresh, language into our hymnal? Would these women's voices allow us to become more open to the Divine?

My first response was to trust these voices and to shape their images and thoughts into hymn texts that could be sung. After all, I had been invited to do that. And as I proceeded, I sensed that I had been "found." What was missing for the hymnal committee was also missing in me. Their gift to me was the opportunity to create out of the writings something I had not sought.

As I completed the three texts and offered them to the committee, I returned, in a sense, what I had been given. In the process I had also found what had been lost. Although I had not been searching, others had, and something valuable was restored. My text "Mothering God, you gave me birth" was sent to nine composers. Coincidentally, all nine created musical settings in which the E-pitch was predominant. Could this be the "mother pitch," we wondered, the pitch that matches the singing of the pregnant mother's blood flow? The chosen musical setting by Janet Peachy is a lovely chant-like tune in E minor. Its setting nurtures me in deep spaces, as if it had always existed and was waiting to be discovered.

JULIAN OF NORWICH, WHO WROTE "ALL WILL BE well, and all manner of thing will be well," lives on in her visions and poetry, and it turns out that I was one of many who drink from her stream. She was born in 1342 in the region of Norwich, England. Little is known of her life aside from her writings, and even her name is uncertain; the name Julian comes from the Church of St. Julian in Norwich, where she was an anchoress. At the age of thirty, suffering from a severe illness, she had a series of intense visions of Jesus Christ. These continued until she overcame the illness, after which she recorded the visions, then again twenty years later. The first version, called *The Short Text*, is a kind of narrative. *The Long Text* contains more theological commentary on the meaning of the visions. These visions are the source of her major work, *Sixteen Revelations of Divine Love*, which is believed to be the first book written by a woman in the English language.

Julian wrote during a time of turmoil, when current events included the Black Death and numerous peasant revolts. While many believed that God was punishing the wicked, Julian's visions led her to believe in a God of love and compassion, reflected clearly in her writing. She believed, too, that the Trinity expressed "mothering" in its very nature.

In the fifty-ninth chapter of *Showings* (*The Long Text*), Julian summarizes her reflections on the Trinity this way: "I understand three ways of contemplating motherhood in God. The first is the foundation of our nature's creation; the second is his taking of our nature, where the motherhood of grace begins; the third is the motherhood at work. And in that, by the same grace, everything is penetrated, in length and in breadth, in height and in depth without end; and it is all one love."

MOTHERING GOD, YOU GAVE ME BIRTH

Mothering God, you gave me birth
in the bright morning of this world.
Creator, Source of every breath,
you are my rain, my wind, my sun.

Mothering Christ, you took my form,
offering me your food of light,
grain of life, and grape of love,
your very body for my peace.

Mothering Spirit, nurturing one,
in arms of patience hold me close,
so that in faith I root and grow
until I flower, until I know.

She continues to make references to the mothering qualities of Jesus especially, mentioning in chapter
sixty how he offers his body as food. These writings
became the source of the hymn text, "Mothering God,
you gave me birth." At the end of chapter sixty-three,
Julian sums up her theology of Christ as mother with
the famous words, "All will be well, and you will see it
yourself, that every kind of thing will be well."

In 1972 I spent three weeks in England with my
family. We settled into an apartment of friends at the
Mennonite Centre in London, and from there we rode
trains to see the famous sights of the country. One of
these trips took us to Norwich to visit friends who were
active in the Church of England and who took us on
a tour of the city, pointing out the anchorhold where
Julian had lived. This was twenty years before I read
her visions as a foundation for a hymn text. At the time
my life was filled with mothering—our four children
traveling with us were ages fifteen, thirteen, nine, and
one. In retrospect, I was seeking ways to lean on God's
mercy and love to carry me as the family grew. When
these words of Julian found me, I received them as
a gift of new identification and strength for my own
spiritual journey.

<hr />

HILDEGARD OF BINGEN WAS BORN IN GERMANY IN
1098, the tenth child of a noble family. As was custom-
ary with the tenth child, she was dedicated as a tithe to

the church. Early in childhood she experienced waking visions, and at age eight she was sent to live with Jutta, an anchoress who led an ascetic life, shut off from the world inside a small room adjacent to a church. During the next thirty years Hildegard confided her visions only to Jutta and a monk named Volmar, who recorded them. Her first book, the *Scivias*, was written over a period of ten years and was affirmed by the bishop and the pope.

Hildegard's contribution to liturgical poetry and music was large. In her lyrical cycle, *Symphony of the harmony of heavenly revelations*, she celebrates her belief that the human soul is "symphonic," that we possess an inner accord of soul and body in human music making. She produced sixty antiphons, responsories, sequences, and hymns. Her poetic language was unusual in medieval European lyrics, her imagery sometimes echoing the mystical love in the Song of Songs. And she demonstrated poetic freedom with daring mixed metaphors, superlatives, exclamations, and intellectual innovation. The effects are often strange or violent and never smooth like her contemporaries. Often her description of the divine is given in feminine terms describing Eve, Mary, and Church-as-Mother as essential figures in God's plan for the redemption of the world.

Mystic and abbess, she founded two monasteries for women, produced seven books on medicine, theology, herbology, biology, botany, and two biographies of saints. Her influence was felt throughout Germany and parts of Gaul. She spoke to people of all classes and walks, exhorting to reform and to heed prophecies and divine warnings entrusted to her.

Hildegard's songs were written in Latin as part of the liturgy for nuns, and the musical settings were her own composition. The words for my adaptation of her texts come primarily from *Antiphon for Divine Wisdom* and *Antiphon for the Holy Spirit*.

O HOLY SPIRIT, ROOT OF LIFE

O Holy Spirit, Root of life,
Creator, cleanser of all things,
anoint our wounds, awaken us
with lustrous movement of your wings.

Eternal Vigor, Saving One,
you free us by your living Word,
becoming flesh to wear our pain,
and all creation is restored.

O Holy Wisdom, Moving Force,
encompass us with wings unfurled,
and carry us, encircling all,
above, below, and through the world.

Some years before I wrote this text, my husband and I walked the streets of Bingen. It is a pleasant village on the Rhine where tour boats offer their passengers a place to visit the shops and cafes. I remember the ubiquitous cuckoo clocks and wooden toys, nothing grand to suggest the life of this amazing woman. The Rhine itself, with its ancient, forceful flow over which the banks tower with rocks and castles, where eagles spread their wings and cry out, was much more representative of her.

⚬

MECHTILD OF MAGDEBURG WAS BORN IN SAXONY circa 1207 to noble parents. At the age of twelve she claimed that she was greeted by the Holy Spirit. She became a Beguine in 1230 and lived in a Dominican convent with its discipline of intense prayer and austerity for forty years. In 1270, after her severe criticism of clergy and extraordinary spiritual experiences, she left and sought refuge in a Cistercian abbey at Helfta, where she was warmly received by Gertrude the Great and Mechtild of Hackeborn.

Mechtild's writing began in 1250, was completed in 1270, and was collected and distributed by friends under the title, *Light of my divinity flowing into all hearts that live without guile.* The original work in Low German has been lost. But translations into South German and Latin are extant. Her writing consists of poems of mystical experience, love songs, visions, and more reflections and admonitions. She borrowed language and imagery from the Song of Songs and sometimes she used the dialogue of minnesingers.

While her work lacks theological content, her mystical doctrine has been described as "sound." My choices for a hymn text were taken from "The Soul," who answers the Youth, who is calling to her to dance, and from the Youth, who explains how he was given instructions by the Trinity for the dance. I also included a few lines from her poem 19: "The manifold mission of Love," which begins: "O blessed Love, whose mission was and is / to unite God and the human soul, / That shall be thy mission without end, / As it was without beginning."

The title of my hymn text "I Cannot Dance, O Love," has been labeled as "the most Mennonite title in the hymn book," since the long tradition of forbidding dancing was part of our heritage. This medieval mystic, so in love with God, gives us permission to dance, literally and metaphorically. This dancing is described as "lifting, circling, and growing beyond all knowledge." Could it be that the dances I used to do in the kitchen to entertain my small children sprang from this source?

I cannot dance, O Love

I cannot dance, O Love, unless you lead me on.
I cannot leap in gladness unless you lift me up.
From love to love we circle, beyond all
    knowledge grow,
for when you lead we follow to new worlds
    you can show.

Love is the music 'round us, we glide as birds
    in air,
entwining soul and body, your wings hold us
    with care.
Your Spirit is the harpist and all your children
    sing;
her hands the currents 'round us, your love
    the golden strings.

O blessed Love, your circling unites us, God
    and soul.
From the beginning, your arms embrace and
    make us whole.
Hold us in steps of mercy from which you
    never part,
that we may know more fully the dances
    of your heart.

In 1991 after my husband and I had toured Poland with a Mennonite history guide, we rented a car in Berlin and drove west to meet my cousins who had immigrated from Karaganda a few years before. As we entered newly liberated East Germany, we came to a sign that marked the city of Magdeburg. Having just written the hymn text a few months before, I exclaimed my interest in driving into this city. The buildings were black from Communist industrial rule, but we did find the cathedral, quite bare, and no reference to Mechtild. I found a janitor who acknowledged her, and said that while the cathedral held no remembrances of her (she had, after all severely criticized the clerics), there was a small museum in the center of town in her honor. Although it was closed, we did confirm that once a deeply inspired young woman was born in this place. And the fact that she had written in the language of my forebears, Low German, seemed significant, for she, too, was writing for the people of her time and place.

A CHRISTIAN MYSTIC HAS BEEN DEFINED AS ONE who achieves knowledge of God through direct awareness or personal intuition, not logic or reasoning, one who desires to realize truth and ultimate meaning, not just think it. This definition is related to the work of writing poetry as well as living a life with God. I was found by the writings of these women as I found what had been lost and hidden, and I continue to be in that process.

The work of Hildegard gave me new names for God and new ways to imagine God's creative, unfathomable acts. The creative acts of humans draw from this source. In the work of Mechtild I found permission to name God as my Lover, the one who holds me in the dances of life and allows me to grow "beyond knowledge." According to Mechtild's language, I am permitted to use the feminine gender for God, moving me into a new freedom. The writings of Julian allowed me to dare to acknowledge God as mother. Julian claims that our longing for God is reciprocated by God's longing for us. I want to learn with Julian to delight in that desire. Like her I want to write our truth, as Grace Jantzen wrote, "a God according to our gender" in our post-modern world. With Julian I want to recognize what in the centuries of patriarchal domination is contrary to God. Her sheltered life in an anchorhold did not become a tomb, but a womb, as she spoke out against violence. She invites me to become a space of natality, to creatively discern and respond to the deathly structures of modernity "so that we may be endlessly born."

A parable is like women's work—contextual and concrete. It sees the ordinary and everyday as the place where God is revealed. The parable of the lost coin is set in a house. The woman is probably poor and needs to burn precious oil in her lamp to search her low, dark house. When she finds the coin she calls her women friends (as indicated in the original Greek) and neighbors to celebrate with her. In 1985 this parable was the theme of the first large conference of women in South America who were part of the liberation theology movement. The coin symbolized a coming together and discovery of selves in light of their experience with God and their work in theology, all of it transformed into a festival.

This parable is one of three—the lost sheep, the lost coin, and the prodigal son—told by Jesus in response to questions from the Pharisees. Why did he eat with sinners? The sinners were those who did not follow the rules of Judaism, the ones outside. These stories all hold the invitation to welcome and include those sinners with festivity. As one who grew up hearing these parables interpreted as primarily a call to be saved from sin, this enlargement of the idea of kingdom offers a deeper and wider space in which to receive its secrets.

The three mystics continue to find me as I learn to open my mind, heart, and body to God. They free me by their visions and fervent love for God, and their courage to challenge the status quo, energizing me to continue to speak on behalf of women restricted by tradition. With their convincing boldness, they give me strength to speak for gays and lesbians who are barred from church membership and for all people who are powerless to live lives freely in this world. Because the writings of these women were preserved by others who recognized the power of their visions, their words and melodies are now in our hands and hearts.

12

My Mother
in Venice:

The Power of Art

1975 to the Present

> She had another life,
> not only the vast expanse
> of prairie, but this island
> adrift and shimmering.
>
> Here she is, in the Frari Church
> holding the Child.
> Centuries ago Bellini
> saw her at the fish market

shivering in the rain,
brought her to the small
fire of his studio
and began brushing her round

face into glow, dressing her
in blue silk—my mother
in this city of mirrors
where the centuries swirl

together, where she still holds
the Child, my Brother,
where she doesn't hold me.

WHEN MY HUSBAND AND I TRAVELED FOR THE
first time to the Soviet Union in 1975, we were taken
to the Tretyakov Gallery in Moscow. After the glittering chapels and palaces of the Kremlin, the spaces and
paintings seemed intimate and shadowed. No bright
Matisses here, but the earthen tones of peasant scenes,
as I remember, and the gory glory of battles. What
caught my heart was the Virgin of Vladimir, the icon
given as a gift from Constantinople after Vladimir converted to Christianity in the eighth century. I had seen
numerous icons, those "windows to prayer" that are
part of Orthodox worship, but this one was different.

In spite of the usual frontal, flat affect of the figure, this one held the melancholy and tenderness of Mary in the tilt of her head and the black of her eyes. And the Child's face pressed high against her cheek seemed to become part of hers, his eyes gazing up at her. Since that journey I have kept a print of the Vladimir on my kitchen windowsill.

A child of Mennonites with centuries of adherence by both maternal and paternal lineage, I had been disconnected from visual arts as part of faith and worship. Our churches had clear glass windows, sometimes in Gothic shape, and a large, carved wooden plaque of scripture text arched over the choir. But images, candles, statues, or stained glass were unacceptable. We were part of the iconoclastic reformation.

My mother's maternal ancestors came from Holland and Germany. The Klassens were Mennonite converts from Holland who fled persecution to northern Germany and Poland in the sixteenth century. The original movements to the Vistula River area occurred at the invitation of those in power at the time. The need for farmers to bring skills for draining the swamplands on both sides of the river brought a number of Dutch Mennonite immigrants who were also given the freedom to practice their objection to military service.

My mother's paternal ancestors carried the name Schultz. Some were farmers and blacksmiths, and a few were town mayors or leaders. When my father married my mother, her brother reminded him that he was marrying aristocracy. Such connotations mattered little in our small rural communities in Saskatchewan and Minnesota. What mattered was hard work and a simple, peaceful way of living. No popes, finery, or confession booths. No candles in church. Then why did I love this icon and want it to be a part of my daily life?

The Mennonite communities in which my husband and I had grown up were not closed. Public schools offered music, drama, and visual art, as did the colleges connected to our churches. But not until our first years of marriage in Chicago, where Louis attended medical school, did we immerse ourselves in viewing art. There the Chicago Art Institute offered us their fine collection for our enrichment—*American Gothic*, straight out of the Midwestern plains, and the Monet lilies glowed for our wonder and pleasure. In those first years we also were exposed to the history and theology of our Mennonite heritage as we shared apartment living with Mennonite seminary students. Our home churches had moved away from their unique history to become a part of the evangelical stream. We were part of an integrated church on the south side of the city, worshiping and learning with those who wrestled with the demands of the gospel, how to live and follow the teaching of Christ. We were awakened to the possibility that art and faith carry deep rivers of connection, that Christ's call to follow in his way would allow an image or object to enliven our imaginations toward deeper, stronger faith.

As charter members of a church here in Fresno, we have encouraged artists in our congregation to create work for our sanctuary and the space around it. Banners, paintings, and sculpture enrich our observance of the church year. Perhaps this incorporation of art and worship is one way to reclaim the land as our ancestors had done. After all, the poetry and parables of scripture glow with birds and bread and trees, and the instructions for the decoration of the temple are vivid with colors, textures, bold artifacts, and pomegranates. Mennonite churches are slowly growing in their honor of the arts in worship, yet we are far from the "smells and bells" of high liturgy, and portraits of apostles and saints are few. We are learning to honor our senses, but Mary is mostly absent except at Christmas. She waits.

She was waiting for me in Venice. Touring in that magical, sinking city in the 1990s, we absorbed the watery life, squinting into the reflected light from bell towers and churches. All of it amazing and "other," until we ventured into the Frari Church, where several grand Titian paintings are installed. Beyond the nave is a side chapel, and there she was, as altarpiece, my mother holding the Child Jesus. Unlike many Italian madonnas with long, slender faces and blonde hair, this one by Bellini had the sweet round face and brown hair of my mother. She matched the image of my mother in a studio family photograph in which she holds her first daughter in her lap. Here she was in a city threatened by floods, like her ancestors, "alive" and glowing.

In the poem I say "She had another life," as she did, that inner center of my mother who held on to the story, the Child, for she couldn't hold us. In that shining and threatened city, she no longer waits. I have arrived to see her dressed in yards of blue silk that she never owned. The Child is a toddler standing on her lap. He is looking off to the side. He will get down and walk away to his own life and death, but she will follow him. She will never give him up. Mary and my mother. Each of us who holds him, and who "like the serene Madonnas of Giovanni Bellini, with their hints of crucifixion ... assure me of two things: first that things are worse than I know, and, second, that they're all right."*

When I worked on the poem that opens this chapter, I struggled with its ending. What was true for me? Was Mary as my mother holding only the Child, whom I claim as Brother, or was she also holding me? As I end this reflection, I choose to revise the ending of the poem — "my mother / in this city of mirrors / where the centuries swirl / together, where she still holds / the Child, my Brother, / where she also holds me."

For I am convinced that by holding the Child, she is holding me and my children and their children. As the mother of God, she holds us all.

* Peter Schjeldahl, *The New Yorker*, Nov. 5, 2007.

Sources

Flinders, Carol Lee. *A Little Book of Women Mystics.*
New York: HarperCollins, 1995.

Haight, Amanda. *Anna Akhmatova: A Poetic Pilgrimage.*
New York: Oxford University Press, 1990.

Hirschfield, Jane, editor. *Women in Praise of the Sacred.*
New York: Harper Perennial, 1995.

Jantzen, Grace. *Julian of Norwich.* Great Britain: The
Cromwell Press, 1987 and 2000.

Massie, Robert K. *Nicholas and Alexandra: The Classic
Account of the Fall of the Romanov Dynasty.* New
York: Random House Trade Publications, 2011;
originally published 1967.

About the Author

JEAN WIEBE JANZEN WAS BORN IN SASKATCHEWAN, WAS raised in the Midwestern United States, and now lives in Fresno, California.

She completed her undergraduate studies at Fresno Pacific University and received a Master of Arts at California State University of Fresno. Collections of her poetry previously published by Good Books include *Three Mennonite Poets* (1986), *Snake in the Parsonage* (1995), *Tasting the Dust* (2000), *Piano in the Vineyard* (2004), and *Paper House* (2008). Her verse also has been collected in *Words for the Silence* (Center for Mennonite Brethren Studies, 1984) and *The Upside-Down Tree* (Henderson Books, 1992).

She was selected for The Creative Writing Fellowship from the National Endowment for the Arts for her poetry.

Janzen's poetry has been published in *Poetry, Gettysburg Review, Prairie Schooner, Image, Christian Century, Poetry International, The Common Reader, The Great River Review,* and *Cincinnati Poetry Review.*

Among the poetry anthologies in which her poems appear are *A Cappella: Mennonite Voices in Poetry* (University of Iowa Press), *Highway 99: A Literary Journey Through California's Great Central Valley* (Heyday Books), and *What Will Suffice: Contemporary American Poets on the Art of Poetry* (Peregrine Smith Books). She also is the author of *Elements of Faithful Writing* (Pandora Press), essays based on a series of lectures delivered at Bethel College in North Newton, Kansas.